The Serenity Principle

The
Serenity
Principle

FINDING INNER PEACE IN RECOVERY

Joseph V. Bailey

HarperOne
An Imprint of HarperCollinsPublishers

HarperOne

THE SERENITY PRINCIPLE: *Finding Inner Peace in Recovery.* Copyright © 1990 by Joseph V. Bailey. All rights reserved. Printed in the United States of America. No part of this book may be used or reproduced in any manner whatsoever without written permission except in the case of brief quotations embodied in critical articles and reviews. For information, address HarperCollins Publishers, 195 Broadway, New York, NY 10007.

HarperCollins books may be purchased for educational, business, or sales promotional use. For information, please e-mail the Special Markets Department at SPsales@harpercollins.com.

HarperCollins Web site: http://www.harpercollins.com

HarperCollins®, ❦®, and HarperOne™ are trademarks of HarperCollins Publishers.

Library of Congress Cataloging-in-Publication Data
Bailey, Joseph V.
    The serenity principle : finding inner peace in recovery. / Joseph V. Bailey. — 1st ed.
        p. cm.
    Includes bibliographical references.
ISBN: 978-0-06-250039-7
    1. Alcoholics—Rehabilitation. 2. Peace of mind. I. Title.
HV5278.B35   1990
362.29'286—dc20   87-46195

18 19 20 21 22 RRD (H) 42 41 40 39 38 37 36

To the serenity and wisdom
within us all

CONTENTS

PREFACE

As a young boy growing up in a small Minnesota town in the 1950s, I felt happy, loved, and secure. There was plenty of time to enjoy life. My buddies and I spent countless hours playing in the barns and the buildings of my dad's nursery, living in a world of make-believe and adventure. I loved to explore the woods as Davy Crockett or Robin Hood. Sometimes I would lie in the tall grass on a hillside overlooking the Mississippi River and dream as I became lost in the images within the clouds as they lumbered by. I didn't have a care in the world. As I look back, I realize I lived in a natural state of serenity during my childhood.

As my life went on I experienced peace of mind less and less often. In my Catholic military high school I felt woefully inadequate to compete in academics, sports, and social life. I began to feel insecure, threatened by life. Try as I did to overcome my inadequacies I always felt insecure. I spent the next twenty-some years trying to regain the feeling I once had known so well.

At first I searched for peace of mind in the acceptance of others. I became quite popular in high school, but I still felt insecure. Then I searched in religion and joined the seminary for a year, but I became disillusioned because my church didn't seem to follow its own principles. In college I began to pursue psychology. It was fascinating to read all the theories of why people feel insecure. I became a psychologist and earnestly tried to apply these theories. But they offered no real answers to finding happiness. I became adept at analyzing myself and others but I didn't help anyone find peace of mind—not even me! As a matter of fact, I felt worse.

Since traditional psychology didn't seem to be the key to serenity, I began to search in the realm of esoteric philosophies and metaphysics. I learned to meditate, practice yoga, and eat whole foods. I experienced moments of that familiar boyhood joy, but it took a lot of work and the feelings never lasted. I searched in too many ways to recount here but the result was basically the same. I kept thinking that the truth was just around the corner. It never was.

One day a dear friend called me about a new breakthrough in psychology that had helped him and his clients immensely. I was skeptical. I had come to believe that the answer was that there are no answers. With the ulterior motive of seeing my friend and escaping the Minnesota winter for warm Florida, I attended a seminar on what is now called Psychology of Mind in November 1980. There I met philosopher, Syd Banks and professionals who were bringing his insights to their fields.

I recognized in the feelings and words of the people there what I had been seeking all those years. At first, what they talked about insulted my intelligence. It was far too simple! But something deep within told me that they made absolute sense. My ego fought for a while because these principles appeared to contradict everything I had spent the previous fifteen years studying. But as my own life changed for the better and my counseling clients responded in new and positive ways, it became clear that I was onto something of true value. I was feeling more and more serene. My clients began to get "well"—not just to recognize their addiction and cope, but to enjoy true peace of mind. In the early 1980s I quit searching outside myself for serenity; I realized it was within me all along.

The principles of Psychology of Mind are based on these premises: the mind is the creator of reality; consciousness and thought work together to create our experience; and we have the power to control thought. By understanding the principles of thought, separate realities, levels of consciousness, and emotions we are empowered to create sane and serene lives.

Psychology of Mind is revolutionizing the fields of mental health, social work, nursing, and related helping professions. Hundreds of professionals who have been trained in this Health Realization Model are experiencing truly transformational results with their clients, results that have never before been seen in our field.

The field of addictions is no exception. I have worked in the addiction field for the past fifteen years as a counselor, teacher, prevention specialist, and consultant. Now many chemical dependency and other addiction counselors are using these principles in their work. As a result, addicts are learning to be free of their compulsions and are enjoying new contentment. And my colleagues are less plagued by stress and burnout.

Through clinical experiences and initial research of Psychology of Mind, we are gathering data to launch psychology's first major psychotherapeutic breakthrough. Numerous studies are showing consistent and lasting outcomes via this approach. The purpose of this book is to introduce this breakthrough to people struggling with addiction, and to those who want to go beyond merely coping to find happiness and peace.

This book is intended to help guide you to an understanding that will open the door to your own wisdom. This understanding is *The Serenity Principle*. It unites the principles of Psychology of Mind and their application to addiction. *The Serenity Principle* offers the means for self-discovery. Remember, you are your own teacher. The words and concepts in this book can help you listen to yourself better. But don't just take my word for it. Listen to what your own life teaches you and see if *The Serenity Principle* makes sense.

ACKNOWLEDGMENTS

Seventeen years ago Mr. Sydney Banks went through a transformational experience. His realization has spawned revolutionary insights by numerous professionals in disciplines as diverse as psychotherapy, nursing, business, and medicine. I feel fortunate to be one such person. I am grateful to Syd Banks for his consultation over the years that helped me realize what I now understand about the human experience and in particular addictions. I also thank the clients, students, and staff at the Minneapolis Institute of Mental Health, whose support was always a source of growth and change.

Thanks are due to those who helped me put my thoughts and feelings into words. Tom Grady, from Harper & Row, encouraged me to write this book and worked with me throughout the editorial process. Caroline Hall Otis helped me make my writing simple and clear; I am grateful for her many hours of editing—what she called "polishing my gem." I thank Darlene Stewart, whose ideas and suggestions helped ensure the integrity of the book. And credit goes to Jane and Eric Malenfant, Jean Kantor, and Jan Gunterious for their clerical assistance.

Finally, I want to acknowledge those closest to me. My parents' unconditional love and happiness have always been an inspiration. And I could not have written this book without the support and wisdom of my wife, Michael. She served as midwife to *The Serenity Principle* by reviewing my writing and helping me be true to myself. Through their love, Michael and my son Ben give me the greatest joy life can bestow.

Chapter 1

INTRODUCTION:
WHY SERENITY?

Serenity, which is the immunity to all addictions, is characterized by feelings of tranquility, gratitude, contentment, affection for others, and a deep inner peace. When people are serene, they don't need to fulfill desires to feel complete. Addiction is the innocent attempt to find completion in a substance or situation. In fact, it can only be found within.

The feeling of serenity is innate. When we "lose" serenity, the desire to regain it is innate as well. For some, that desire is quickened by adversity or physical/emotional problems. For others, the search represents curiosity about the deeper meaning of life.

Throughout the brief history of addiction treatment, various leaders have stated that the antidote for addiction is serenity, a spiritual awakening, a changed level of consciousness. Until recently, this has been easier said than achieved. Today, understanding the applications known as Psychology of Mind map a clear path to this goal.

When we open our hearts and minds, our inner wisdom is revealed. Open-mindedness is, in fact, the key to personal evolution and growth. It is the fertile soil where insights germinate. An insight is a thought that occurs to an individual while experiencing serenity. The mind is the origin of thought and consciousness; it creates the power to formulate thought and is the source of all wisdom. (It is a greater intelligence than our individual mind.)

For growth to occur, it is important that you stay open-minded when reading this book. Temporarily set aside your previous ideas, even those that have helped you. Fixed ideas will only block your ability to learn something deeper. Humility—the realization that "I can learn something new"—opens the door to listening, which in this context means allowing the words to reach beyond the intellect. Call it intuition or inner intelligence. Listening can occur only when the mind is quiet. When we filter what we read through our beliefs, we block out a portion of what is being said, so don't try to analyze your problems as you read—it will only keep your mind busy and prevent you from realizing your inner wisdom.

Serenity is like electrical energy. We can't see it directly, but we can see its tangible effects in light, heat, appliances, and machines. We don't need to understand what electricity is or how it works to benefit from it. We need only plug it in and turn it on. It's the same with serenity. When we understand the principles of how to realize serenity, we are able to plug into the energy that lies within.

Before I understood the principles of psychological functioning in my own life, serenity was a theoretical construct, a goal that I might attain for a few moments if I worked hard enough. Now my life is filled with contentment, peace of mind, and gratitude. I hope that you, too, will realize these principles in all aspects of your life.

The Results of Serenity

Serenity is our birthright. The ability to experience this is as natural to us as breathing or digesting food. When we are in a state of physical health, those functions are balanced. In a healthy mental state all our emotions, thoughts, and behaviors act in unison, too. We experience harmonious interaction with our environment.

The ramifications of living in a state of serenity are far-reaching and profound. Serenity changes every aspect of our lives. In the same way that a single match illuminates darkness, a glimpse of serenity changes how we see every aspect of our existence.

One obvious manifestation of serenity is mature, harmonious human relationships. When we feel serene, we are more open, honest, respectful, and loving. There is no need for defensiveness or blame. We can see and appreciate the positive characteristics of others. When others are feeling insecure and behaving negatively, we can respond with compassion and patience. We feel no need to control them so that we can feel good. Above all, we see the best in others, a vision that allows them to realize their inner goodness, too.

Happiness fosters learning; insecurity or fear hinders it. When we are in a state of serenity, our ability to listen, learn, and create is enhanced. The tranquil mind is an open channel of perception and insight, spurred by curiosity, unobstructed by past beliefs, attitudes, limitations, and prejudices.

When we are serene, we are excited and motivated to contribute. Work is a joy. We are more productive with less effort, and free of stress, able to see positive solutions to problems.

Our minds and bodies are inseparable. Modern medicine shows a causal relationship between state of mind and the body's immune system, growth and development, physical attractiveness, and organ function. When we are in a positive mental state, we get sick less often, heal more quickly, and enjoy our bodies more.

When we are serene, we can more easily realize the full potential of our talents and relationships. Living in the present, we are no longer plagued by guilt, resentment, and fears.

Serenity lets us access our wisdom. We see life objectively and gain more freedom of choice.

Clearly, serenity has many benefits. If our sole purpose for pursuing it is to gain these benefits, however, then we have put the cart before the horse. Serenity comes first, above all other things. Our quest must take a turn away from the illusion that external events create our happiness. The source is deep within, and that is where our focus must be.

The key to achieving serenity is found in the elements of the three principles of psychological functioning. In part 1 of this book, I explain the important elements that will help the reader to begin to experience serenity. First, however, we must understand the nature of the addict's search.

Chapter 2

THE SEARCH FOR SERENITY, THE COMMON DENOMINATOR OF ADDICTIONS

We all search, knowingly or unknowingly, for the positive feeling that lies deep within. Some call it happiness, others peace of mind; still others call it the search for love. When we experience this sensation, it is like coming home after a long journey. We are safe, secure, and at peace with the world.

Becoming addicted to drugs, alcohol, food, sex, gambling, or any other substance or circumstance represents an innocent, often desperate search outside ourselves for a positive feeling. Advertisers sell everything from perfume to cigarettes by promising a reasonable facsimile of happiness. When we don't understand how or where to find serenity in our lives, we are compelled to seek it through whatever means we believe will work.

If we don't experience happiness in our lives, we feel unbalanced, empty—as if something were missing. We hunger for something to fill the gap, and we tend to look for it outside ourselves. This state of desire provokes many negative emotions that may be summed up as "insecurity." Insecurity is characterized by feeling out of control and dis-eased. It is an unnatural state that makes us susceptible to addictive habits. Insecurity can take form as shyness, competitiveness, hostility, arrogance, defiance, intellectualizing, showing off, and more.

I used to work in drug abuse prevention, where I learned an important lesson. We told people all the harmful effects of drugs and assumed they would listen to reason. The secure and happy kids would listen and avoid drugs, but the unhappy kids used them no matter how great the risk. I have worked with people who sniffed glue, drank cleaning fluid, shot up with dirty needles—the search for serenity has little to do with reason. Because there were a lot of unhappy kids, our prevention program backfired and drug abuse mounted. Clearly, providing information was not enough.

Regardless of the addictive habit, its root is always the same—the need to feel good. If you cut off only the top of a weed, such external behaviors as alcohol abuse or gambling, the weed will always grow back if the root remains intact. In our efforts to prevent and treat addictions we have tended to focus on specific external behaviors (the top of the weed)—the alcohol abuse, the eating disorder, the gambling. This is one reason why so many "recovered" addicts relapse or swap one addiction for another. Some people even get addicted to self-help groups or books. I recently heard a woman introduce herself at an

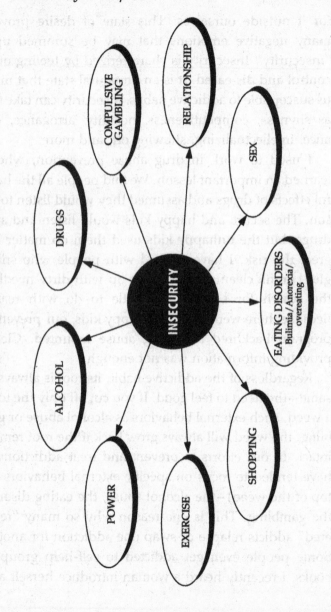

The Common Denominator of Addictions

INSECURITY

COMPULSIVE GAMBLING

RELATIONSHIP

SEX

EATING DISORDERS
Bulimia / Anorexia / overeating

DRUGS

SHOPPING

ALCOHOL

EXERCISE

POWER

AA meeting with five different addiction labels. She was going to seven Twelve-Step meetings a week plus therapy, and she still wasn't happy. In truth, all addictions are manifestations of the same disease—insecurity.

In the 1970s there was a heated debate in this country about whether or not to combine the treatment of alcoholism and drug addiction. At the time, various addictions were treated as separate diseases. It was apparent, however, that the processes of substance addictions were similar, so we came up with the umbrella term "chemical dependency." Later, people began to wonder if chemical dependency treatment methods could be applied to other dependencies, such as food and sex addictions, gambling, and shoplifting, to name a few. Soon specific networks developed for each of the growing number of addictions.

To understand addictions we don't need more information about an endless variety of substances and the harmful effects of each. We don't need more people specializing in treating specific addictions. What we do need is an understanding of the common denominator of all addictions and the common antidote to feelings of insecurity, emptiness, and unhappiness. The solution, mental health and serenity, will come with simplicity, not complexity.

Once upon a time there was a man who spent his days searching for happiness. With intense dedication he pursued answers in every new pleasure and accomplishment, but found none. Having exhausted every source of happiness he could think of, he decided to look in the opposite direction. I will look in hell, he thought. I will find out why everyone there is so unhappy. This may give me a clue to happiness. He was transported to the gates of hell in an instant. Lucifer welcomed him and assured him that once his curiosity was satisfied he could leave whenever he wanted.

To his surprise, hell was identical to earth. The only difference was that *everyone* was unhappy.

He was persistent in his quest. He interviewed hundreds of hell-dwellers for several days, trying many approaches. He talked to all types of people but they could not tell him exactly why they were so miserable. Then one day a desperately unhappy woman pulled him aside and said, "You'll see!" Her words disturbed him deeply. Although he had not come up with any answers, he decided to leave.

He returned to the gates of hell and saw a sign he had not noticed before. It read: "Before leaving hell you must satisfy these three conditions . . . " He felt trapped, but the conditions seemed easy enough to satisfy. He remembered Lucifer had said he could leave at any time.

He set out to complete the first task. When he returned he noticed that the first item had been crossed off, but the list had grown by one. His fear started to take over. But then he had a brilliant idea. He had always prided himself on his speed and efficiency. He would memorize the three remaining conditions and quickly fulfill them, freeing himself from hell. Thinking he had outwitted the devil, he set out to complete his requirements.

He approached the gate again and found that he had outsmarted no one. In fact, the list was four conditions longer. He was devastated by the pressure to complete the ever-growing list. Days went by. His thinking was no longer clear. He felt trapped by an overwhelming mountain of details.

Overcome by exhaustion, he fell into a deep sleep and dreamed he was collapsed at the gates of hell, wanting to leave and live his life in peace. In desperation he stood and reached for the handle. The gate was not locked.

The shock of his dream awakened him. "Of course it was only a dream," he thought. "That solution would be too simple. But what if it were true?" He chastised himself for even thinking that life could be so easy. "Forget it, I'm doomed. I'll never get out!"

But the memory of the dream persisted, bringing with it a feeling of hope. The hope was stronger than his fear of disappointment. "What could it hurt? . . . Maybe I'll try . . . It might be that simple." He reached out and grasped the handle. It turned. He realized that he had the power to be free whenever he chose, and knew he had found his answer.

Each of us must realize, as did the man who went to hell, that we already have the solution we seek. It is to be found in simplicity.

The answer lies in an innate state of mind that is deeper than intellectual intelligence: wisdom. Wisdom guides us to use our thoughts well and leads us to serenity. To find wisdom, we must understand how the mind functions. This understanding doesn't lie in the realm of thinking. It is not merely intellectual; it is inspirational.

The next section of this book outlines four important elements of Psychology of Mind, our map to this inner wisdom. When we truly desire serenity we will learn to listen to our instinctive direction and follow the map. Our inner hunger will be satisfied and we will no longer need to search outside ourselves for peace of mind.

The Serenity Principle

PART ONE

The Serenity Principle

Chapter 3

THOUGHT—THE CREATOR
OF OUR UNIVERSE

The three principles that make up Psychology of Mind provide a remarkably simple and concise understanding of how the mind works. These are the three principles: 1) Thought forms our psychological experience. It structures how each of us views the world. 2) Consciousness makes our thoughts appear real. 3) Mind is the source of consciousness and thought. For practical purposes, our mind is what we think with. In this chapter and the three that follow, I describe the elements of each that are important in recovery.

The Function of Thought

Life is as it appears because of how we think it to be. Thought is our greatest gift. It is the very creator of our psychological experience; we cannot experience life without it. Modern perceptual psychology has discovered that seeing, hearing, smelling, and all other sensory experience occur in the brain, not in the eyes, ears, and nose.

The brain decodes incoming sensory signals to fit its cognitive hypotheses, or hunches, imposing order on a chaos of information by organizing it according to past expectations and experiences.

As we go through life we are always expecting, perceiving, and interpreting our experience through our thoughts. Our senses selectively "let in" that which corresponds to our interests and prejudices. Take, for example, the experience of a man driving a car down the road. He sees the road and other cars; he especially notices older cars because he is a collector. His wife, a gardener, sees people's yards and notices all the plants. Meanwhile, his father in the back seat is preoccupied with financial problems and notices only the signs of an eroding economy, such as closed businesses. Each of them perceives reality selectively.

We are always thinking. William James, the father of American psychology, called this the stream of consciousness, because thinking is never-ending though it has many forms and an infinite variety of contents. Even though thought creates every ounce of our experience, most of us are unaware that we are thinking and that we are free to control the content of our thoughts.

Consequently, we tend to blame "outside reality" for negative experiences, and this makes us feel powerless and unhappy. When we realize that we are in control, we can change our thoughts and create a more satisfying reality. This is known as free will.

Thought Systems

As each of us goes through life, we store all our experiences in what becomes a personalized thought system, the software of our bio-computer, the brain. The brain processes data into concepts, beliefs, and opinions that make up our present frame of reference. Although each thought system is unique, all operate according to a uniform set of principles, just as mathematical laws apply regardless of the variables in the equation.

The thought system is known as the ego or personality in most psychological theories. This becomes the filter through which we interpret life. The thought system behaves like any ecological system, striving to maintain a balance, supporting the status quo. In other words, we look for and see whatever validates our pre-existing view of reality. We innocently forget that we are creating the thoughts and become personally identified with the content of our thinking—our beliefs, values, and ideas.

What we are thinking at any given moment, consciously or not, creates our experience of reality. Our interpretation of what our senses are telling us creates an emotional response. Our emotions, then, are not caused by outside events or people; rather, they are a direct result of our perception. For example, people who like skiing are delighted when it snows; others are depressed because they hate any sign of winter. The snow itself doesn't cause these reactions.

We express emotion through physiological changes, tone of voice, and body language. These behaviors catalyze reactions from other people, and in our own bodies. Of course, other people's reactions are generated through their interpretation of our behavior. We interpret their responses through our own thought system. Thus, the thought system is self-fulfilling and self-validating. The diagram on the next page will help illustrate the process.

If I believe that Mondays are depressing, when I wake up on Monday I have already preprogrammed the day. I go to my closet and think I have nothing to wear. "If only I could lose a few pounds, these clothes would fit me." Traffic seems to crawl as I drive to work. I begin to feel rushed and, as I start thinking about all I have to do that day, the momentum builds. Angry now, I honk my horn at a driver who forgets to signal. When I can finally step on the accelerator, I get a speeding ticket. Now the day is ruined for sure!

Everyone at work seems to be in a bad mood, especially my boss. I have to do more than I deserve or can handle. I procrastinate and make mistakes. "I knew I should have stayed in bed this morning!" Thus, my self-fulfilling prophecy about Mondays is validated again.

When we are unaware that our thoughts create reality, we become victims of our belief system and can only respond through our habits. This is the concept of sincere delusion. Our moods are dictated by the day of the week, other people's moods and behavior, the weather, the stock market, or anything else that we deem important.

The Dynamics of Viewing External Reality
Through a Personalized Thought System

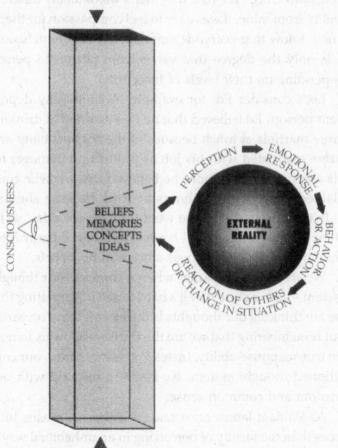

A deluded person doesn't realize that he or she, not the weather, is in charge.

I used to judge alcoholics to be different, weaker, and morally inferior until I understood the concept of sincere delusion. Once I realized that theirs was a totally different reality from mine, it was easy to feel compassion for them. I now know that everyone suffers from sincere delusion; it is only the degree that varies from person to person depending on their levels of insecurity.

Let's consider Ed, for example. A chemically dependent person, Ed believed that he was justified in drinking three martinis at lunch because of the responsibility and stress associated with his job as production manager for his company. In addition, he believed that his wife complained about his long hours at work because she just didn't understand what he went through each day, so he often stopped by the local bar to avoid her. Ed may have been misguided, but he was sincere in his beliefs.

We are like fish in water when it comes to our thought system—it is so close that it's hard to see it. Forgetting that we are thinking our thoughts is the easiest thing on earth. But remembering that we are the thinkers allow us to realize true response-ability. Instead of reacting from our conditioned thought system, we begin to respond with our wisdom and common sense.

As William James once said: "Genius . . . means little more than the faculty of perceiving in an unhabitual way."[2]

Have you ever had a "serious" problem that had you so worried, confused, and full of negative emotions that you couldn't figure it out? After getting away from your problem—perhaps through a good night's sleep or a visit with a close friend—suddenly you had an insight. The solution seemed obvious. This is an example of wisdom at work.

Paradoxically, when we momentarily forget our problems, or release our grip on negative thinking, our view shifts to a higher, more objective perspective. Consider this analogy: if you focus on the smashed bug on the windshield of your car, you will definitely miss the scenery and likely have an accident. Wisdom is like looking through the windshield, not at it.

When people are attached to their thinking, they seldom have insights. Instead, they get bogged down in their problems, unable to tap their wisdom. Insights occur when the mind is quiet, not busy.

Wisdom is a state of mind. We can't try to be wise—we already are, naturally. When we are in this state, we see life objectively and learn more quickly, without the interference of insecurity. We readily love and share intimacy with others. We communicate easily because we listen to others and to our hearts instead of depending upon a set of beliefs.

"God grant me the serenity to accept the things I cannot change, the courage to change the things I can, and the wisdom to know the difference."[3] As the Serenity Prayer implies, serenity is a prerequisite to the state of mind known as wisdom.

Many recovered people sense intuitively the connection between serenity and wisdom. Understanding how the mind functions—particularly how thought works—makes that link very clear.

In *The Wizard of Oz*, Dorothy ultimately found that the home she sought had never left her. It was in her heart all along. We, too, will ultimately find what we seek, not by thinking and planning and analyzing, but by listening softly to the wisdom within.

The next element, that of separate realities, will help us to better understand the thought principle. All three principles are interwoven. Each gives a fuller picture of the whole.

Chapter 4

SEPARATE REALITIES

When I was sixteen years old I lived for three months with a family in Central America. Coming from a rural American community in the Midwest, I was in culture shock for the first two weeks. My Guatemalan family's view of reality was totally different from mine in terms of what they liked to eat, the way they expressed emotions, their politics, family values, dating customs, sense of humor, work habits, and more. At first I was shocked and judged their differences as bad, or even sick. I felt homesick for people who saw "reality" as I did. But as time went on I began to appreciate and even envy their way of looking at life. They seemed to enjoy life more, expressed their love more openly, and were more relaxed. When I returned to Minnesota, I tried to get my family to act more like my Guatemalan family!

This experience showed me for the first time that reality has many faces. My frame of reference reflected my upbringing and conditioning rather than any absolute truth. This shift in perspective widened my appreciation and compassion for people of all walks of life and cultures and freed me from my fear of things that didn't jibe with my personal frame of reference (or thought system).

No two people live in the same reality. There are, of course, certain broad cultural and familial similarities, but extreme variation exists even within these groups. For each of us, our personalized thought system creates a unique reference through which we view and experience our own reality.

Your TV set offers evidence of separate realities. Thanks to the networks, cable, and satellite, you can see many regional and international interpretations of the same sporting event, racial incident, farm, or environmental issue. If you listened to coverage of an international event in different countries—say in two nonallied Middle Eastern nations—you would hear very different versions of the "facts." The newscasters are all sincere in believing that they are objective and balanced, but they seem to be talking about entirely different events.

When we acknowledge separate realities we can look beyond our own frame of reference and drop our negative biases and judgments. We recognize our own conditioned beliefs and take our thoughts and the thoughts of others less seriously. We attach less self-esteem to whether or not others see eye to eye with us. When we see our frame of reference for what it is, we can appreciate it without identifying with it. This allows us to enjoy people who see life differently without being threatened. Viva la difference!

Within each person there are many different realities.

Separate Realities

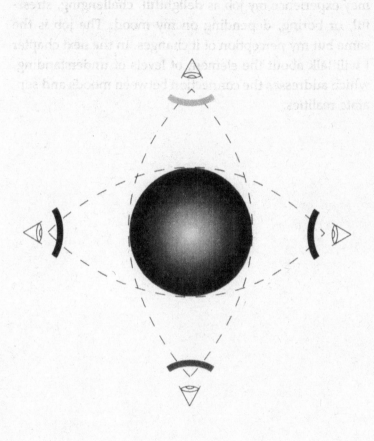

What determines how I experience reality from moment to moment is my mood or state of mind. For example, I may experience my job as delightful, challenging, stressful, or boring, depending on my mood. The job is the same but my perception of it changes. In the next chapter I will talk about the element of levels of understanding, which addresses the connection between moods and separate realities.

LEVELS OF UNDERSTANDING

When we are flying at low altitudes, clouds or fog often obstruct the view. We have limited time to react and are more likely to make mistakes. As the plane ascends we can see farther and have adequate time to plan and respond, thus avoiding danger. And then there's that beautiful moment when we break through the clouds into the sunlight. Similarly, as our level rises, we break through to our natural wisdom and common sense. We can handle life's problems and decisions with ease.

A high level of understanding is nothing more than a good mood. Everyone likes to feel good. In a good mood we have more fun, accomplish more, and get along better with others. We can transcend our habits, compulsions, and insecurities and be ourselves. We are more objective about our world.

Conversely, when we are in a low mood, our world narrows. We become preoccupied with our thoughts and live within the confines of our frame of reference.

If I wake up in a bad mood, my wife looks less attractive and my son seems bratty. It may not dawn on me for several hours that I'm just in a bad mood and am not seeing very clearly. For some people, that realization may never dawn. On the other hand, if I wake up in a positive mood, I think, "I'm so lucky to be married to my beautiful wife and my son is a wonder!"

The only difference in these two situations is my level of understanding. A higher level of understanding is characterized by positive feelings, good concentration, high productivity, enjoyment of everyday activities, strong self-esteem, and good decision-making ability. A low mood is often associated with irritability, defensiveness, a tendency to take things personally, and low productivity. In this state we feel rushed and under stress, overwhelmed, bored, and restless. We experience symptoms of emotional imbalance such as insomnia, anxiety, and depression. It is in lower levels of understanding that we click into the thought system that triggers our learned habits and addictions. We turn to the negative coping habits that lead to a downward spiral. It is here that we need to remember that our thought system is untrustworthy.

In higher levels of understanding, we remember the source of our thoughts and we feel less compelled by their content. In a lower level of understanding, we "fall asleep" and forget that we are doing the thinking, turning to circumstances outside ourselves for help.

Recently an alcoholic client had an experience that illustrates this process. George had been out of alcoholism treatment for four months and was just beginning to get

Levels of Understanding

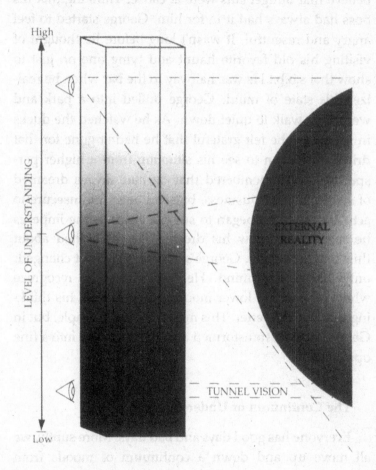

his life in order when he was informed that due to budget cuts, he would be laid off. His mood plunged. He didn't believe that budget cuts were at cause. Thinking that his boss had always had it in for him, George started to feel angry and resentful. It wasn't long before he thought of visiting his old favorite haunt and tying one on just to show that s.o.b.! He was halfway to the bar when he realized his state of mind. George pulled into a park and went for a walk to quiet down. As he watched the ducks in the pond, he felt grateful that he hadn't gone for that drink and began to see his situation from a higher perspective. He remembered that he had always dreamed of starting a new business, but had been too insecure to actually do it. He began to see the layoff as the impetus he needed to follow his dream. He felt excited about this new possibility. George's situation had not changed, only his state of mind. He had learned to recognize when he was in a lower mood and to distrust his thinking until he felt better. This may seem quite simple, but in George's case it transformed a possible relapse into a fine opportunity.

The Continuum of Understanding

Everyone has good days and bad days. More subtly, we all move up and down a continuum of moods from moment to moment. Defining "high" and "low" is purely subjective: one person's highest moment is another's average experience. As we realize this understanding at a deeper level, we still experience mood shifts, but we no longer feel controlled by them.

When I first learned Psychology of Mind, I was acutely aware of my level of understanding. I was self-conscious and frustrated each time I was in a lower mood. When I was in a higher mood I became pleased with myself and felt a little superior. I thought I should be on a high level all the time now that I "knew" the principles. As you can predict, I felt worse and began to feel stuck. That's why it is important to see our moods impersonally. Certainly, we would prefer to be in a higher mood, but it is in trying to change our lower moods that they persist.

The Dispassionate Nature of Moods

When I saw that my mood swings were a force of nature, I learned to flow with them rather than try to control them. Say, for example, that we are sailing. A storm comes up and the winds are fierce. Common sense tells us to drop our sails or find a safe harbor until the storm passes. If we don't, we will tear our sails or capsize. When the winds are right, we can hoist the sails and enjoy ourselves again.

Psychologically, when we recognize our lower levels of understanding, we need to drop our sails, quiet down, let go of our thoughts, and listen to our wisdom. It will tell us exactly what we need to do to ride out the storm and return to a higher level. This may feel like a passive approach, but it is potently passive. Just as you must yield to the rhythms of the ocean current in order to return to shore, so you must yield to the ebbs and flows of mood to return to solid ground. When we stop picking at our problems and slow down, we regain our perspective and can often laugh at how silly we were. We accept ourselves.

Recognizing a mood drop is like running over the lane division bumps in the highway. They tell us we are off track; we can be glad we ran over them rather than smash head-on into another car. Our wisdom signals a dropping mood. If we don't heed the warnings, we will drop further and experience increasing emotional discomfort until we "wake up." Sometimes we end up in the emotional ditch first.

As we internalize this idea, we can catch ourselves earlier and spend less time in the ditch. For the recovering person this is a very important understanding. Studies of all types of addictions show that people usually relapse when they are in a negative emotional state. When we understand how our moods work, we are better able to avoid those lower levels where habits and addictions feel compelling. Rather than fuel the fire with thinking, we can retreat from our thinking and let the flames die out. Realizing levels of understanding is a key to serenity in our lives.

The next element reveals how emotions function as built-in delusion and mood detectors. Emotions help us to recognize our moment-to-moment level of understanding and let us know when our thinking is self-defeating.

Chapter 6

EMOTIONS— OUR BUILT-IN MOOD AND DELUSION DETECTORS

The human body has a feedback system that alerts us to our present state of physical health and balance. It lets us know if we are hot or cold, hungry or satisfied, tired or needing exercise. It also lets us know, through pain, if we are sick or injured. Without this feedback, none of us would survive very long.

The body has a similar mechanism that monitors our mental health: our emotions. Emotions alert us to our present state of psychological functioning. When our level of understanding is high, our emotions are positive and we feel serene. Conversely, when our psychological functioning is at a low level, our emotions are negative. We feel hurt, stressful, sad, angry, jealous, irritated, and confused. These feelings let us know that it is time to listen to our common sense and stop thinking. If we try to analyze our emotions, we will inevitably engage our conditioned thought system and spiral down in levels of understanding. We will become less conscious of our ability to control thought and more conscious of the content of our thoughts. This usually leads to blame, projection, and looking outside ourselves for solutions to our problems. It's like struggling in quicksand. The more we think, the lower we sink.

If the engine gauge flashes "hot" while we are driving down the highway, common sense tells us to pull over, turn off the engine, and figure out what's wrong. If we continue to drive, the engine could blow up. Most of us wouldn't notice the problem if we didn't have gauges because the engine is hidden from view. So it is with thought—it is out of view until it has already done considerable damage. That is why listening to the safety gauge of our emotions is so important. When we learn to listen to our negative emotions and psychologically pull off the road, we will avoid many potential problems in life. If we are feeling positive, we are probably headed in the right direction.

Can you imagine what would happen if you didn't have gauges in your car, or you ignored them, or you thought that a flashing red light meant all systems go? Your car wouldn't last long. In many ways, what we have been taught about our emotions by current psychological theory is just like that. Helping professionals tell us to get in touch with our feelings and express past resentments, guilt, unresolved issues of grief, and trauma. We are told that if we don't do this, they will fester and explode. It is true that if we ignore our feelings we will harm our bodies, relationships, and productivity. But if a pressure

The Emotional Feedback System

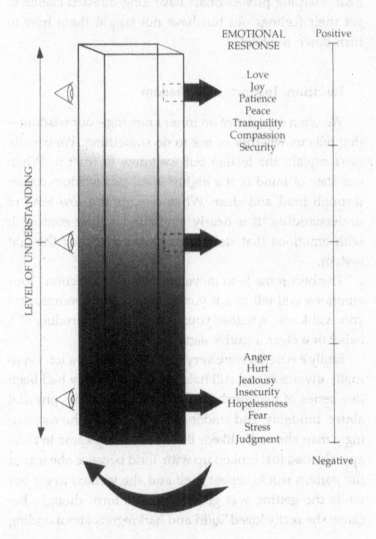

EMOTIONAL
RESPONSE

Positive

Love
Joy
Patience
Peace
Tranquility
Compassion
Security

Anger
Hurt
Jealousy
Insecurity
Hopelessness
Fear
Stress
Judgment

Negative

LEVEL OF UNDERSTANDING

cooker is ready to explode, you can simply turn down the heat. Helping professionals have long directed clients to get their feelings out but have not taught them how to turn down the heat.

Intuition, Instinct, and Wisdom

We often experience an inner knowing—our wisdom—that tells us whether or not to do something. We usually can't explain the feeling but we know to trust it. When our state of mind is at a higher level, this wisdom comes through loud and clear. When we are at a low level of understanding, it is nearly inaudible and we confuse it with emotions that stem from our conditioned thought system.

The best route is to move in a positive direction. Your emotions will tell you if you're on the right course, and you will know whether your feeling is a by-product of a belief or a clear intuitive signal.

Emily's parents were very insecure, argued a lot, eventually divorced, and still hate each other. Emily had been in a series of relationships that always ended in physical abuse, infidelity, and emotional pain. Finally she was dating a man she really liked. But when Emily came to therapy, she had just broken up with Todd because she feared the pattern would repeat itself and she wanted to get out while the getting was good. She was torn, though, because she really loved Todd and had regrets about ending the relationship. She felt depressed, confused, and hopeless about ever having a happy relationship.

As she began to understand the principles of Psychology of Mind, Emily felt happier, hopeful about her life, and less preoccupied with her decision. She began to see how her insecurities had led her to keep Todd at arm's length, making him insecure enough to seek the company of other women which, of course, validated Emily's belief system.

One day, Emily ran into Todd and was surprised at how much affection she felt for him. Now she knew to trust and follow her positive emotions. Low moods continued to activate her old feelings of jealousy and fear, but she learned to ignore them and let Todd know she was just in a bad mood. He responded with kindness and support that helped her feel better.

Emotions are the inner signals that alert us to unhealthy psychological functioning. Without emotions, we are psychologically flying in the dark. With them, we have the radar to navigate smoothly.

The next section of the book deals with the implications of Psychology of Mind for addiction and recovery.

Psychology of Mind and Addictions

PART TWO

Psychology of Mind
and addictions

Chapter 7

TWO-DIMENSIONAL RECOVERY

A decade ago, as a psychologist working with addicted persons and their families, I felt frustrated by what I considered to be inconsistent and unsatisfactory results. Conventional wisdom had it that recovery was a lifelong, often difficult struggle. Clients needed to face the many issues they had avoided through their addiction. Most of my clients were overwhelmed. They clung to me and/or their support group while they tried to wade through these issues. Some gave up and returned to their addiction. Others developed a new compulsion to replace the one they had left behind. Still others developed emotional problems such as depression and anxiety.

I became adept at "fixing" their problems or referring them to the appropriate specialist. Thanks to many workshops, I was proficient at diagnosing codependency, adult children of alcoholics, incest victims, and others. The goal of helping my clients to realize mental health or happiness became obscured by my preoccupation with their problems.

The negativity was overwhelming; I felt burned out. Most of my colleagues were experiencing the same stress, so I thought I was normal. We gathered in support groups to commiserate about our profession and try to come up with ways to cope. I learned to meditate, keep a journal, do guided imagery and yoga. I exercised regularly. None of these cures had lasting effects. I knew something was missing. I kept searching. I tried to improve my skills as a therapist by learning new techniques and strategies, reading books, and attending seminars. I considered finding a new profession or doing less direct client work. Looking back, I had put a cap on what my clients and I could expect from life. I didn't believe it was possible to enjoy continuing mental health or serenity. That would be denial!

Many health care professionals and clients face the same dilemma today. But I got lucky, for as you know, I found an understanding that let me and my clients experience mental well-being without long, painful therapy.

Up until now, psychology has offered us a one-dimensional view of human beings. This view sees the individual as a personality that is shaped by past conditioning and genetics and can be neatly categorized according to an ever-growing list of labels and diagnoses. Treatment is focused on reliving the past, getting out negative feelings, and coping via various rituals and techniques.

The two-dimensional understanding of human beings characteristic of Psychology of Mind offers a more hopeful view. It sees human beings as capable of self-awareness, with an innate ability to transcend determinants of past and biology by becoming aware of moment- to-moment psychological functioning. The focus of treatment is on health, growth, and happiness.

This educational process reveals that the source of power to change is within our own minds. By understanding thought, separate realities, moods, and emotions, we can move to two-dimensional psychological functioning that transcends our habits and patterns of thinking. The result is increased mental health, freedom, and an internal sense of response-ability for our lives.

In this chapter, I discuss the implications of Psychology of Mind for the process of addiction and recovery. I explore the two dimensions of recovery from addictions—the first based on changing belief systems (one-dimensional) and the second based on changing the level of understanding of one's psychological functioning (two-dimensional).

The Formation of Habit

The cornerstone of any addiction is habit. The dictionary defines habit as "an acquired behavior pattern regularly followed until it has become almost involuntary." We all have thousands of habits: we brush our teeth morning and night, fasten our seatbelts when we enter the car, start the day with a cup of coffee. Habits can be as simple as tying our shoelaces or as complicated as flying an airplane.

Learning a habit involves a complex process of conditioning and shaping. My mother spent years reminding me to brush my teeth, to wash my hands before eating, and to acquire many other social skills. While learning a habit we are conscious of it. Tying our shoelaces was once tedious and difficult. After we mastered it, we did it automatically—without thinking.

Habits are difficult to break because once they are formed, we don't consciously think about them. That's by no means all bad. Imagine if every time you drove a car you had to think out each step? You would never get anywhere on time or enjoy the scenery. Our habits save time and effort.

We learn many useful habits that promote physical health, safety, communication, athletic skills, and so on. We also learn some that are harmful to our well-being, such as smoking cigarettes, eating junk food, being controlling and argumentative, and other more serious behaviors. Sometimes we change our negative habits when we realize that they are harmful to ourselves or others. When I started smoking cigarettes there was very little talk about their potential danger and, besides, all my friends were doing it and I wanted to gain their approval. It wasn't until smoking had become ingrained that I realized how harmful it was. By then it was very difficult to quit but with some effort I accomplished it.

Habits that are difficult to stop and seem out of our control are called addictions. An addiction is a habit pattern that is repeated despite its consistent harmful consequences. We can become addicted to virtually any habit we associate with a feeling of well-being—alcohol, drugs, eating, relationships, sexual behaviors, gambling, working, running, shopping, cleaning house, physical abuse, and so many more. Each day we hear of yet another program started to treat another type of addiction. The list of addictions will undoubtedly grow because of our infinite creative capacity to seek a positive feeling. We have been called an addictive society; the term is well-earned. But how and why is it that we develop addictions?

From Habit to Addiction

For a negative habit to become an addiction we must live consistently in a lower state of understanding. We must be dissatisfied with life to be susceptible. This state of mind is called insecurity. When we are insecure we lack serenity and mental health. We don't know to look within, so we search outside ourselves for a positive feeling to fill the void.

At a low level of understanding, we lack common sense about where to find positive feelings. A starving person will eat almost anything. A person who feels lost in life will adopt any habit that he or she thinks will help, even if it has harmful effects. For example, an insecure adolescent will succumb to peer pressure to use alcohol or drugs, or to participate in illegal behavior, more readily than will a secure peer.

A person in a low mood is looking for a way to raise his or her mood. Substances such as alcohol, marijuana, and crack alter moods. These drugs may also confer social acceptance and an artificial sense of self-esteem. When we have a cold, we take antihistamines to relieve the symptoms. We aren't cured, but we feel better. We would never take antihistamines if we didn't have cold symptoms because we would only feel the negative side effects of the drug. The same is true when it comes to mood-altering substances—we don't want to alter our mood if we like the mood we're in.

For example, I once saw an adolescent client who had run away from home, was using drugs, was unmotivated in school, and was very angry at his parents and society. After hearing about Psychology of Mind, he immediately recognized their wisdom. He had been through chemical dependency treatment twice, but had resumed drug use when he was released. After his first session with us, he smoked marijuana a couple of times but found that it dulled his newfound feelings of well-being. Since that time he has not used drugs or alcohol because he has no desire to. His relationship with his parents is better than it has ever been, and he is excited about school and is getting excellent grades.

Persons at a low level of understanding perceive that they are victims of circumstance. They have negative emotions such as stress and low self-esteem. It is as if they are physically run down and thus are vulnerable to colds and viruses. In this weakened state they are susceptible to "catching" negative habits.

If these persons try crack, they will experience the drug as extremely positive and euphoric. Unaware that the source of positive feelings is theirs to control, their mood will be raised temporarily. This momentary euphoria may lead them to become conditioned to the habit of using crack (or any mood-altering substance or circumstance). Their perception of the positive effects of the drug will be maximized and they will ignore the negative effects. Their thought system will form a belief about the habit that is self-sustaining and resistant to change. The legal risks, cost, and social consequences will be lost in a complex web of rationalizations, while the blissful feelings hold sway.

The Spiral of Addiction

Once the negative habit pattern of an addiction is ingrained, the person will remember positive perceptions of the drug whenever his or her mood drops. This creates urges and preoccupation with thoughts of the habit. The addict's priorities in life gradually begin to shift toward the addiction and away from relationships, health, job, and school. Increased use brings more extreme mood swings—from elation to paranoia and depression. The addict starts to live on an emotional roller coaster. Self-esteem drops and increasingly the addict looks to the object of addiction for positive feelings.

As the habit becomes more compulsive, its negative consequences increase—loss of friends, distance from family, divorce, legal difficulties, financial problems, and, ultimately, physical deterioration. In the case of some substances (such as alcohol), the addict may experience increased tolerance, blackouts, distortion of memory, and physical withdrawal when not drinking. As the addiction progresses, the level of understanding continues to drop and the person experiences fewer of life's natural joys. The addict feels more and more out of control and less aware that the problem is his or her own thinking and behavior. In the later stages of addiction the person's life may deteriorate to the point of despair and suicide. Premature death from accident or illness is common.

Progression of the addiction is marked by decreasing awareness of thinking as a voluntary ability, increasing negative thoughts and feelings, and dysfunctional behavior. This sad downward spiral is a reality to millions of people throughout the world.

One-Dimensional Recovery

The traditional understanding of psychological functioning sees present behaviors as a product of past experiences, heredity, and learned patterns of behavior. The client is seen as diseased, in denial, manipulative, and unmotivated to change. Treatment consists of confronting addicts' negative behaviors, breaking down their defenses, helping them get in touch with negative emotions, continually recalling their past mistakes, and focusing on the addictive symptoms and pathology. The goals of treatment are to help addicts admit that they are sick and powerless to control their disease, learn to cope with chronic illness, deal with unresolved psychological issues, and commit to attend support groups for the rest of their lives in order to remain abstinent and obtain peace of mind.

One-dimensional recovery has helped numerous addicts return to health and productivity. It has undoubtedly saved many lives. But all in all, it doesn't work very well. As one client of mine put it: "I'm sober but not sane." Sustained abstinence requires effort and constant support. A recent report in the *New York Times* indicates that the average AA member attends four meetings a week.[4]

One-dimensional recovery works to change addicts' belief systems without increasing their understanding of psychological functioning. This approach tends to make them dependent on new belief systems rather than on their own powerful inner resources. Their thinking often becomes belief-laden and rigid. Addicts must constantly remind themselves of their past for fear of repeating it. They still have the urge to practice their original addictive habits or new ones, but they keep it under control through their new belief system. They feel they must identify themselves with their illness or their guard will slip and they may suffer a relapse. Their self-esteem is conditionally based on how well they are "working their program" and other external factors.

Serenity is the goal of one-dimensional therapy, but it is seldom realized on any consistent level by most recovering people. For consistency to occur, addicts must change their level of understanding enough to maintain balance in their lives. Otherwise, they have changed just enough to quit the addiction but not enough to be happy.

Two-Dimensional Recovery

Two-dimensional recovery is based on a deep understanding of the nature of the mind and the principles by which it functions. It incorporates and goes beyond a one-dimensional view of human beings—their genetics, past, and learned behaviors—to an awareness of levels of understanding. Two-dimensional recovery encourages the addict to identify with the unlimited creative power that lies within each of us. The assumption is that each person has the ability to return to the innate state of natural serenity. Negative, addictive behavior is attributable to insecurity and a low level of psychological functioning rather than to weakness or disease. This approach recognizes the elements of separate realities and thus defines people's manipulation and denial as the way they are experiencing reality through their unique thought system. Two-dimensional recovery assumes that a person is not sick but lacks understanding that thought is a voluntary function and thus acts in ways that are self-defeating and harmful to others.

Two-dimensional treatment is a guide to higher levels of understanding. The focus is on helping the person feel safe and lighthearted, for positive feelings will lead the way to serenity and full recovery. The treatment is non-judgmental; it educates in a nonthreatening way.

The primary goal of two-dimensional recovery is learning to live in the moment by dropping memories and limitations and learning to find positive feelings of serenity within.

The Spiral of Recovery

Two-dimensional recovery promotes unconditional positive feelings and natural self-esteem. It frees people from destructive habits while it enables them to tap into their own common sense and wisdom for a life filled with joy.

The key difference between one-dimensional and two-dimensional recovery is that the second delivers an insight into the nature of thought: we are the creators of our own reality. This insight begins a transformation that continues as a process of realizations about the nature of life.

The compulsions that filled our thinking during one-dimensional recovery are replaced by feelings of joy, self-esteem, love, and tolerance for others. Recovery is no longer a struggle, but an experience of increasing fulfillment. Little by little we drop thoughts of the past and our addiction and see ourselves as whole human beings. Our moods begin to stabilize. Even though we experience normal ups and downs, the downs don't last nearly as long. We don't take them seriously, nor do we dwell on negative thoughts that perpetuate our low moods. We use common sense to take better care of physical needs and

**Spiral of Insecurity
and Addiction**

**Spiral of Freedom
from Compulsion**

Negative thought
is taken as real

Increased insecurity

Increased desire

Inner conflict

Habits are
triggered

Temporary
relief

Guilt and shame

Feelings of powerlessness
and compulsiveness
are reinforced

Lowered self-esteem

Controlling

Letting Go

Serenity
Free choice

Spontaneity

Wisdom
Understanding

Clarity

Peace of mind

Slowed-down thought

Feelings of
security

Feelings of tranquility

Insight
about thought

Acceptance

develop positive habits of living. Insecurity is replaced with an unending curiosity about life and enjoyment of its wonders. Our natural ability to be intimate and loving leads to healing of old relationships and development of new, meaningful friendships. We are able to help others through example, patience, compassion, and gentle guidance.

Two-dimensional recovery is a possibility for everyone, not just for the lucky few. As I reflect on my own life and the many clients I have known, I think of the corresponding transformation that occurs in nature. Through the process of metamorphosis an earthbound caterpillar becomes a free, airborne butterfly. Through understanding, people who have been enslaved to their thoughts are freed to soar into a life of freedom, unending hope, and serenity.

Chapter 8

THE MYTHS OF RECOVERY

When we come to understand the principle behind any process, we can perceive the myths or misconceptions that shaped our previous thinking about it.

Over the brief history of the treatment of addictions, professionals have developed numerous beliefs about what is necessary to recovery. Early on, we believed that AA was the only way an alcoholic could be helped. This gave way to the notion of inpatient treatment; soon inpatient treatment of twenty-eight days became the magic formula. This idea is now giving way to acceptance of outpatient treatment as a more economical and effective means to recovery.

Much of current addictions treatment is based on one-dimensional assumptions from earlier psychological theories, as discussed in the previous chapter. Such thinking sees the human being as the product of biological and environmental determinants. It doesn't take into account the fact that people can transcend these influences through changing levels of understanding, the two-dimensional approach.

I do not condemn the work that has been done in addictions to date. The tendency to turn thought-created insights into immutable beliefs is common in every field of science. It is yet another example of how thought systems become self-validating and self-limiting. The time has come, however, to take the next evolutionary step toward the truth. And one day, this "truth" must give way to an ever-deepening understanding of the human mind and its functions.

Now, let us look at how some current myths contaminate our efforts to recover from addictions.

MYTH #1: *It is important to become aware of, discuss, and express negative thoughts and emotions in order to recover from addictive behaviors.*

If I have a leaky canoe, I need to bail to keep from sinking to the bottom of the lake. If the holes in the canoe are our negative thoughts, traditional counseling techniques have given clients increasingly sophisticated methods of bailing to avert triggering unwanted behaviors. The assumption here is that emotions have a life of their own—that we cannot control but can only try to cope with our emotions. We are forgetting that emotions are created moment to moment through thinking, a voluntary function. If we experience each negative thought as real, we let it generate negative emotions that we feel we must express. The water level is rising. We can't bail fast enough. Wouldn't it be easier to patch the canoe?

Traditional treatment counselors tell clients that they

must learn to get out their anger, sadness, jealousy, and other negative emotions that threaten their recovery. In so doing, they negate clients' power to create their emotions in the first place.

Just as a teapot whistle alerts you to turn off the heat, our negative emotions signal negative thoughts that we need to turn off. (Of course, there are times when it is perfectly natural to choose to dwell on the thoughts that gave rise to your "negative" emotions. For example, when you have suffered a loss, it may feel positive and healthy to cry or feel sad.) When we learn to listen to our emotions as signals of state of mind, we can recognize when we are sincerely deluded by the thinking of our egos. Getting in touch with our emotions is not an end in itself; it is a tool for charting the right course.

MYTH #2: *Understanding and remembering the past is necessary to recover from addictions and to prevent relapse.*

This myth is built on the assumption that the past is real, a fallacy that keeps nations and neighbors at war for centuries over issues that no longer exist.

The past is not real. It was real when it was the present, but now it is only a memory carried through time by thought. Through hypnotic regression or electrical stimulation of the brain, we can get a person to "relive" an experience of the past, but what is played back is not the event; rather, it is the memory of the event. How we interpret the memory depends on our present state of mind.

A memory is like a photograph; every person snaps the shot from a different angle. Ask ten people about the same event and you'll get ten different answers; each person has unique memories and corresponding emotions that add up to ten separate realities.

When I am in a low mood and I remember a past situation, I tend to dwell on the negative parts. When my mood rises, I suddenly see the positive aspects as well. In a higher mood my blinders are removed and I see more of the "whole picture." My level of understanding makes a huge difference in my memories and perceptions.

As a happy-go-lucky child, I didn't analyze my life much. I enjoyed many wonderful experiences and quickly got over the negative ones. Later in life, while studying psychology, I began to search my past for negativity. Guess what? I found it. I saw that I didn't get enough love and that I actually had a very unhappy childhood. This perception led to elaborate beliefs about my family that in turn led to feelings of anger, hurt, and distance toward them. Later, when I began to realize the principles of Psychology of Mind, I saw the same past, but with more understanding and compassion and also with a more complete picture of the whole. I began to feel gratitude for my childhood experiences and true forgiveness for the negativity. Presto chango—a happy childhood!

Recently, a client told me that for forty-seven years she had felt guilty about an event (sexual abuse) that had occurred when she was seven years old. When she began to see that the past was not a fact, but something that could be viewed from any perspective she chose, her feelings of anger and guilt were transformed into forgiveness and compassion. She is now able to feel comfortable with her father after a lifetime of guilt and fear.

The past is an illusion. The power of this simple truth is profound and far-reaching in its implications.

There is an important difference between repression of a past memory, positive thinking, and changing our level of understanding of the past. Repression is the psychological process of denying a thought for so long that we don't even realize we are doing it anymore, yet we still harbor the thought. Repression is like driving toward a brick wall with your eyes closed. Positive thinking is when you try to imagine that the brick wall is actually a tunnel. But when you have a clear understanding of the past, you see the wall and simply drive around it.

From Freud on, treatment, psychotherapy, and self-help groups have placed a tremendous emphasis on the past. Traditional addictions treatment has it that remembering the past is an antidote against repeating it. It forces clients and their families to dredge up every painful detail in an attempt to break down the ego and its defenses. Continuing "drunk-a-logues" remind them of their past and the danger of becoming cocky. The goal is to stay humble and wary of the insidious nature of the disease.

Humility is indeed necessary for continued growth; it keeps us open, listening, and grateful for our insights. Gratitude is the very antithesis of arrogance. But humiliation is not a prerequisite to humility. Humility comes through a change in understanding.

On the road to serenity and full recovery, it is essential to learn to drop the baggage of the past and to move toward the future, the eternal now. Traveling light is always the best way to go.

MYTH #3: *There is no cure for chronic addictions.*

It is a well-established belief that alcoholism and other addictions are chronic—that is, there is no cure, only relief from the symptoms. These ideas are based on the one-dimensional notion that the personality is a fixed and stable entity. We now realize that the personality is the sum of ideas that people believe about themselves, so that the personality changes with different states of mind or levels of understanding.

Just as water takes on different forms at different temperatures, the human personality changes at different levels of understanding. Addictive behavior patterns are triggered at certain psychological temperatures or states of mind. As people evolve in understanding, they no longer find their addictive thought patterns compelling. Even when they temporarily drop into low moods, they are able to see these thoughts as nothing more than thoughts—not as urges that must be fulfilled. This is why many people who were once "hopelessly" addicted now live happy and productive lives.

Of course, if a person abstains from an addiction— gambling for example—without a deep understanding of healthy psychological functioning, a bad mood will bring on the urge to gamble because that is the only way that the person knows to feel better. Once clients have a real change in understanding, however, they will no longer be driven by the old urges because they know how to feel better without their "vice."

A recurring theme in the Big Book of AA (Alcoholics Anonymous) is recovered alcoholics who are rescued from the "compulsion to drink" thanks to a spiritual awakening, the product of the Twelve-Step program. A spiritual awakening is simply a change in understanding, a new awareness that neutralizes the compulsion to drink. Without two-dimensional change—that is, a change in awareness of our own psychological functioning—we are forced to "cope" with the compulsion. The one-dimensional treatment system tries to scare people out of their addiction by telling them that they will always be recovering—never recovered—and that they must constantly affirm this to themselves and others.

A close friend, who used to binge on food, recently told me about her recovery process. It began as she became conscious that she had a problem and sought help. She joined Overeaters Anonymous and, with support from the group, she began to feel hope and gradually overcame her compulsive eating, though she still didn't feel secure. Later, she learned of the principles of Psychology of Mind and said her real recovery began. An understanding of these principles helped her gain peace of mind and she quit thinking of herself as a compulsive eater. She said that dropping the label of compulsive eater—and the identity that went with it—released her more fully from her past behavior.

For many, the label "recovering addict" defines their lives. But we are more than our past behaviors. We are human beings, not human beens. We can choose whether or not to make addictive behavior a reality in the present.

A client expresses this concept eloquently[5]:

Do you have a label for me that says just who I am?
Do you know what's deep inside and everywhere I have been?
Can you see past the teardrops and into my heart,
And realize that I just didn't know where to start?

Will you watch me change, and watch me grow,
And see my candle really glow?
Can you imagine what it feels like to me
When all I really want to do is be?

So you have given me this label
That says sometimes I am unstable,
But you never bothered to look inside
And see that all I wanted to do was hide.

I'm not really who you think I am,
But if you took a moment to hold my hand
I think it would help you to understand.
You see, we are all just learning
Each and every day,
And things are always changing.
Please help me find my way.
I may have made mistakes, but it's just because

I didn't know how to quiet my busy mind and
Listen softly to my soul.

If we are to realize full recovery, we must move beyond "coping with our addiction"—our thoughts—and enter the process at an earlier stage. We need to understand how the mind works in order to live in levels of understanding where substances have no power, avoiding the states of mind where the old addictive patterns are triggered. This understanding leads to serenity, the antidote for relapse.

If we give addiction power by fearing it, fear anchors us to lower levels of understanding, distancing us from a higher, more volitional state of mind.

The notion that we are "victims" of disease, history, or habits is popular in our culture. "I drink because I am an alcoholic." "I can't help myself, I have an addictive personality." Ideas like these rob people of their freedom and sense of responsibility. Remember when Dan White of San Francisco was acquitted of murdering the Mayor and a City Supervisor thanks to the "Twinkie defense"? He believed his addiction to junk food robbed him of the power to control himself. People must be able to act on their own volition—and be accountable for their actions.

The disease concept was a way to inject compassion and humane treatment for alcoholism, drug addiction, incest, and other maladaptive behaviors into our cultural belief system. Moving toward compassion truly helped the profession to evolve. We must now take another step, one that restores freedom and responsibility to our lives.

MYTH #4: *Each type of addiction is unique and only another person with the same illness can effectively treat and understand it.*

People who have freed themselves of "your" addiction represent hope. Hope is a beautiful feeling that alleviates isolation and despair. It carries a person from suffering into a higher state of mind. If, however, we create the belief that only another who is similarly afflicted can understand us, then we are limiting tremendously our sources of compassion and understanding. I have seen people with different addiction labels segregate themselves in the same way that races, nationalities, and religious groups have done for centuries. This prejudice prevents them from seeing the mutuality of human beings and puts a limit on their growth. The more we believe we are unique, the more stuck we become.

There are numerous specific treatment programs based on variations of the addiction problem rather than on the commonality of the solution. This approach is one-dimensional. By concentrating on the details of the problem, we miss seeing that we are two-dimensional beings capable of insight and wisdom. It is true that some people share similar characteristics on the ego level. Our greatest commonality, however, is our uniform psychological functioning. We must look here—not to our differences—for solutions.

It is wisdom that helps others, not understanding of the problem. To help someone who is drowning in quicksand, you must be out of the quicksand yourself.

MYTH #5: *It is necessary to focus on the details and problems of one's life in order to find serenity.*

I have known hundreds of recovering people who suffer from a common ailment—"analysis paralysis." So much of what we have been taught in psychology says we must "work through" our issues one by one. We are often told, "If you're not happy, you had better go to therapy, unearth your unresolved issues, and work through them."

Before I started understanding the principles of Psychology of Mind and how they applied to my life and work as a counselor, I would tell people, "It's going to get worse before it gets better. Facing the issues you have been denying through your addiction will be painful, but the process is necessary for your recovery." I now see that this belief actually glued them more firmly to their problems and issues.

If you are going to clean your house, you don't examine each piece of dust as you go. You simply sweep it away. Similarly, there is no value in looking at all the details of your life; obsessing stalls the promise of recovery—serenity. For example, Judy came to therapy with a list of several major issues she wanted to work on: her anger toward her father and men, her sexuality and intimacy, stress at work, and her phobia of escalators. After a few sessions it became clear to her that her thinking was creating each of her issues. She avoided years of therapy by recognizing the common source of the details that were troubling her. She also quit smoking, which wasn't even a goal.

Every addict's primary addiction is to thought. Addicts are constantly analyzing themselves, as well as others and their problems. This low-level thinking produces the feeling of insecurity that addicts attempt to alleviate through drink, drugs, gambling, and other destructive behavior. If we encourage our clients to dwell on the details of their lives, we are fueling the fires of their insecurity.

And we are missing the point: we created all those details through thought and are still creating them at this very moment, as we choose. Our problems and our past do not cause emotional imbalance and unhappiness. The cause is our thinking. The cure is to understand that thought is voluntary, which frees us to drop negative thoughts and create a new, more positive reality.

MYTH #6: *Positivity is a sign of delusion.*

Harry, a former client, had recently finished treatment with a counselor who had warned him to be wary of the high that typically comes with the end of treatment. He shouldn't trust his positive feelings. The counselor told Harry that he would soon settle back to "normal" life with its ups and downs and that he might begin to experience depression. He went on to say that Harry would need to deal with unresolved issues since he had previously used alcohol to cope with them. In developmental terms, he said, Harry was now about twenty years old, the age at which he had become addicted to alcohol.

Harry was referred to me to deal with family and childhood abuse issues. The counselor's predictions seemed to have come true. Shortly after Harry returned home, his treatment high disappeared and he was indeed depressed. He began to think about all the issues that his counselor said were repressed—his financial problems, his marriage, his broken relationships. He decided it was time to see me and he made an appointment. He came to the first session frightened at the prospect of exploring issues he would just as soon forget. Harry was relieved when I told him that the past was over; he should lay it to rest and learn to start his life anew. I encouraged him to trust his positive feelings. He was afraid at first, but he gradually learned to trust them and his life began to change.

If, as treatment professionals, we direct ourselves and our clients to trust our innate mental health, growth is rapid and direct. If our emotional signals are positive we are headed toward understanding, change, and serenity. If they are negative, we are clinging to a belief—and heading for a low mood where we may get stuck.

Expectations and beliefs are the sculptors of reality. Whatever we expect will be our experience. If we expect recovery to be hard, painful, and lifelong, that is what life will give us. If we learn to still our expectations, we will be constantly amazed at life's gifts. If we learn to recognize mental health and serenity, we will soon see it growing in our lives.

Many recovering people believe that serenity is an illusive prize, attainable only after completing an arduous course. But it does not take time to realize serenity. It is within reach right now. Serenity is something we already have, if we will only drop our thoughts of the past and future.

And we don't even have to try. In fact, trying too hard to figure out how to gain serenity can add difficulty and pain to the process. Trying is precisely what prevents our natural state of well-being from surfacing. You cannot try to feel positive or serene. Serenity is like a cork in water. Weighed down with conditioned thought, it is submerged. When we "let go" of the content of our thinking, we remove the obstacles to our positive feelings.

When many people first hear of these principles, they confuse them with Pollyannaish positive thinking. But positivity is not a thought; it is a feeling experienced when one lives in the now in a higher state of mind. Happiness is not a sign of delusion, but a sign that we are on track.

MYTH #7: *No pain, no gain.*

Long ago, a counselor who was in training with me said she used to see how long it would take to get her groups to break down and cry. She would measure her effectiveness as a counselor by how many tissues she went through each week. She believed that the more people got in touch with their pain, the better they would feel. One of her clients summed it up: "Well . . . as the rabbit said when he made love to the porcupine, I believe I've enjoyed about as much of this as I can stand!" Most of her clients echoed these sentiments.

It must get worse before it gets better. Good medicine has to taste bad. Nothing worth anything comes without hard work and suffering. Who said life was going to be a bed of roses? Somehow, we came to believe that life must be full of suffering and hard work. The more we suffer now, the greater our reward later (in heaven).

The fact that suffering has been the experience of a great many people doesn't make this belief true. Anything is difficult until you understand the principle behind it. When I first tried to ride a bike, it seemed impossible; once I got it, it was a snap. The same is true for finding serenity in our lives. Before we understand the principles behind it, it seems like the most elusive goal on earth. Once we begin to understand, however, what once seemed painful and excruciatingly slow happens easily and quickly.

We have confused the expression of pain with mental health. Like any other negative emotion, pain is a feed-back mechanism that lets us know we are off track. Like the bumps between the highway lanes, pain awakens us to the fact that we are headed for trouble. We must change our thinking or risk a head-on crash with life. Common sense tells us that mental health is a positive feeling. We wouldn't think of physical pain as a sign that we were getting better, but that is exactly what we have done in the treatment of addictions and mental illness. Over the past eight years I have seen clients far exceed the level of mental well-being that I used to hope for. They are no longer just coping; they are enjoying a natural, ever-expanding state of mind filled with new insights, growth, and positive feelings. The best part is that they don't have to endure painful and expensive long-term psychotherapy to achieve this state. Some people realize these principles in just a few sessions. Others take considerably longer. But research findings on Psychology of Mind show that therapy averages just nine to sixteen sessions. And the therapy process is painless and often fun. That should be no surprise, since we learn about serenity and mental health by experiencing it, not by experiencing more mental illness.

We know enough about pain—addicts are experts at pain. What is important is to learn to live life without painful consequences. We may still fall off our bikes periodically, which reminds us that we need to learn more, but we don't have to keep learning by deliberately hitting the sidewalk.

MYTH #8: *Rituals and techniques are necessary to achieve and maintain serenity.*

Two years ago, Sarah completed treatment for cocaine addiction. Since leaving her aftercare group at the treatment center, she has regularly attended Cocaine Addicts Anonymous, Adult Children of Alcoholics, Overeaters Anonymous, and a weekly assertiveness training group. She begins each day by reading three or four daily meditation books, writing in her journal, and meditating for thirty minutes to relax. Then she goes for a thirty-minute jog. She is also using psychotherapy to work through her previous sexual victimization.

Sarah sounds like she is really "working" her program and should get an A+ for effort. For some reason, though, she can't sleep very well, feels a great deal of stress at work, and can't seem to establish a positive relationship in her life. She also feels guilty when exhaustion keeps her from following all her daily rituals. What's the matter with Sarah?

Sarah believes that doing all the right things will make her a happy, well-balanced person. Believing that serenity is something we do rather than something we are is a problem that many recovering people face. They are enslaved to the techniques they have adopted to find full recovery and happiness.

There is nothing inherently wrong in any of the rituals that Sarah follows. Reading inspirational materials is often a good reminder to listen to our common sense. Exercise is beneficial in moderation. But these things cannot deliver consistent happiness.

Serenity comes from within. If we believe we can experience this feeling only by performing certain rituals, then we are creating another addiction.

I recently talked to someone who is addicted to physical exercise. He spends four to six hours a day working out. He is plagued with numerous injuries. He has no time for his relationships and his work is suffering, yet he claims that he really loves exercise and that it is keeping him sober.

Meditation is another technique that is often misused. Meditation puts the ego (beliefs) to sleep, enabling us to access a clear thought channel of inspiration or wisdom. When we are in the state of meditation, we are living totally in the now. The trouble is, many people believe that to experience this state of mind, they must be saying a mantra or performing some other prescribed behavior. They put off experiencing this state until they have time to meditate, not realizing that they can get there at any time under any circumstance.

I used to meditate religiously. I enjoyed it immensely and felt very calm till it "wore off" during the day. I would grow increasingly tense and I couldn't wait to get home and meditate. If circumstances intervened, I would get frustrated and upset. Believing that meditation was in my doing rather than in my being put a limit on when I could experience living.

Our inner wisdom lets us know what to do to stay serene. It tells us what to eat, when to rest, when to exercise, and anything else that promotes growth and health. When we do not trust this inner common sense, we depend on beliefs, rituals, and rules to obtain that positive feeling. Doing these rituals without using common sense is like using an outdated map to find our way in unfamiliar territory. Some entries on the map may still be helpful; others will cause us to lose our way. Our built-in guidance system is 100 percent accurate once we learn to quiet our minds and listen to it.

PART THREE

Living in Serenity

Chapter 9

LIVING WITHOUT STRESS

I used to believe that it was impossible to live in this day and time without a certain amount of stress. Nearly every day the media reiterate that we live in a stressful world. In a recent study by the National Center for Health Statistics, more than half the people surveyed said they had experienced "moderate" or "a lot of" stress in the past two weeks. Some experts put the cost of stress—in terms of lost productivity, medical expenses, and absenteeism—at $150 billion a year, or roughly the size of the federal deficit.[6] Changes in technology, attitudes, and family roles, the threat of nuclear war, job pressures, and economic crisis all appear to be valid reasons for feeling stressed.

Stress seems to have come into our lives like an untreatable virus that can lead to alcoholism, family problems, suicide, mental illness, and physical ailments. Hundreds of programs and techniques, ranging from biofeedback to exercise, have mushroomed to control and cope with stress.

Burnout is the state of mind resulting from sustained stress. It is characterized by loss of motivation; decreased

enjoyment, creativity, and productivity at work; and lack
of energy and desire to continue.

In the addictions field we are told that the average
counselor burns out within five years. Treatment counselors last an average of two to three years in each job.
When you ask why they quit, they often say, "The job was
just too stressful. I had to get out or crack up." Is all this
stress a necessary part of our profession and our lives?
The answer is no. Stress can be prevented once we understand what it is and where it comes from.

What Is Stress?

Stress is a negative emotional and/or physiological
response to a perceived external situation or event. For a
situation or event to be stressful we must perceive it to be
stressful. We create stress through our thinking. When we
believe what others tell us, we accept the emotional consequences. A negative thought that is believed always creates a negative emotion. For example, if I believe that
being a therapist is stressful, I will feel stressed. If I believe
change is stressful, it will be. But if I understand how the
mind functions, I can change my thoughts/perceptions. I
can break the automatic cycle of conditioned thought →
emotion → behavior → environmental response → valida-
tion of conditioned thought. By remembering that I am
the thinker I can choose to buy into a thought or ignore it.
My common sense dictates whether thought is coming
from wisdom or is a replay of old beliefs.

A chemical dependency counselor recently told me that he entered training because he felt so grateful for his own recovery that he wanted to devote his life to helping others. During his training, he was warned that burnout was a fact of life for the profession and that most counselors didn't last more than five years. He didn't want to believe this and hoped it would never happen to him, but he wondered if it were true. When he got his first job, he noticed that the new counselors still cared and had a sparkle in their eyes, but most of the old-timers were tired, angry, and caught up in politics—and were looking for new careers. They teased him about his enthusiasm in an envious way and reminded him that it wouldn't last. Doubts began to creep in that he too would burn out. Then it started. He began to long for vacations and weekends, to commiserate with the old-timers about the patients, the administration, and the lack of respect for his work. Soon he was living out the prophecy of the training program. "They were right," he thought.

This kind of process could have been prevented if the counselor had understood that stress is created by thought. It is a common belief that stress is caused "out there" rather than within our thinking. We can resist this belief only if we realize that it is a myth. When doctors used to tell people they could catch a cold from sitting in a draft, people believed the priests of scientific fact and caught colds while sitting in drafts. In the 1950s when this myth was "disproved," people gradually dropped this belief and the colds that followed it. The medical literature is filled with similar examples of myths and their consequences. What are the myths about stress and burnout?

Myths About Stress

MYTH #1: *Stress is natural and therefore unavoidable.*

A state of stress has become the norm in our culture, so many think it must be natural. Our everyday conversations are riddled with the word *stress*. "I'm under a lot of stress at work." "It's a stressful time of year." "Everything in my life is changing; you'd be under stress too!" Stress has become our most acceptable mental illness. In fact, if you are not under stress in certain situations, it means you lack commitment or are deluded.

But stress is not natural. Serenity is the only natural state of mind because it is present whenever we listen to the Self. You need experience serenity for only a moment to realize that it feels totally natural. Stress is the product of a busy mind taking its own thoughts seriously. Stress occurs when we forget we are the thinkers.

MYTH #2: *Stress is necessary for creativity, motivation, productivity, growth, learning, and development.*

We associate the idea of stress with just about everything that seems to be of value. All high achievers and successful professionals seem to be under stress. We're told that if you really want something, you have to work hard and sacrifice your health, happiness, family life, and lots of other good things in order to put out the maximum effort. This is one path to "success," but it doesn't bring contentment and happiness.

Another, more effective way to be creative, motivated, and productive is through inspiration. Inspiration occurs when the ego is put to rest and we are guided from inside toward the right amount of energy and insight to accomplish more than we believed we could. When we quit trying and the mind is quiet, we are suffused with new ideas and motivated to carry them to fruition.

For example, when I am in a natural state of well-being, writing this book feels effortless and fills me with energy rather than fatigue. When I counsel from that state of mind, my work is filled with love, spontaneity, strength, presence, and magic. Whatever I do in this natural state of serenity I do well, be it gardening, parenting, exercising, or resting.

Fulfillment comes with living from inspiration. When we are guided from within rather than through the "shoulds" of our belief system, life unfolds naturally and perfectly.

MYTH #3: *Developing a high stress tolerance is beneficial.*

We tend to admire people who can tolerate pain and hardship. In the world of addictions treatment, we admire those who can "handle" the stress of our work. The result of this belief has been an extremely high rate of burnout.

As we realize the principles of serenity in our lives, a paradox occurs. Our sensitivity to stress and other forms of negativity grows while our tolerance shrinks. Increasingly unwilling to experience these feelings, we begin to let go of stress-producing thoughts, or nip them in the bud. Our common sense directs us to avoid habits that produce stressful thoughts, such as commiserating with negative thinkers. Rather, we direct our attention toward helping others, improving our environment, and using creativity to make work more positive, humane, and fulfilling. Stress is not something to be managed or tolerated but to be listened to in the same way we listen to physical symptoms that warn us of approaching illness. If I can catch a stressful thought as it enters my mind I can prevent a lot of sleepless nights, irritation, and negative behavior.

Believing that developing a high stress tolerance is beneficial is like believing that being able to run a marathon with a fifty-pound pack on your back is a good idea. Stress is an unnecessary burden we unknowingly place on ourselves. It depletes our energy, stifles our creativity, and prevents us from enjoying positive, serene feelings. Have you ever started driving your car with the emergency brake on? The car is sluggish; you may think you are stuck until you notice the brake. Many of us are driving with our brakes on, believing that life must be difficult. The truth is, when we recognize that we are producing negative thinking, we can release those thoughts, enjoy life, and be productive.

MYTH #4: *Stress comes from the environment.*

A few years back researchers developed stress scales to determine the levels of stress associated with specific life events. After taking the test, my stress level rose because the changes occurring in my life clearly put me in the danger zone.

We have created innumerable beliefs about how life stages, occupations, weather, places, and situations all create stress in our lives. We learn this in school and through the media, friends, and family. Every time we believe these ideas, we innocently allow more stress into our lives. I used to believe that if I wasn't experiencing stress about certain things I must be in denial, so I analyzed myself until I felt appropriately terrible.

A friend once told me an incredible story about a man who should have been under an enormous amount of stress, given his environment. He wasn't. After Germany surrendered at the end of World War II, my friend was sent to the German concentration camps to help the internees return to their homes and reenter normal life. In Auschwitz, he met a man who had seen his entire family and town wiped out by the Germans. The man was spared because he spoke several languages fluently. He was sent to a concentration camp and had been there for five years when my friend arrived.

This man was an inspiration to the soldiers and the other prisoners alike. His energy seemed unlimited, and he always had a smile and an encouraging word for those in need. My friend thought he must have just arrived at the camp because he looked so healthy, unlike countless others who seemed near death. One day my friend asked him how he had managed to flourish during this horrible nightmare. He told my friend that on the day his family was murdered he felt a tremendous hatred for the Germans and wanted to kill them or die himself. Then he realized that this thought made him what his enemies were. He made a conscious decision to love and never to look back. Consequently, he lived one day at a time and found whatever joy he could in helping others to survive. His perception of his environment was radically different from that of his peers, and his physical and mental health showed it.

This dramatic example highlights how our thoughts and perceptions about our environment create our emotions and reactions—not the environment itself.

If we believe it is stressful to be a counselor, a parent, a boss, or whatever, it will be. But it is not the outside circumstance that creates the stress. It is our perception of it. When we realize the power of our perception we can strip off that fifty-pound pack.

MYTH #5: *Change, both positive and negative, is stressful.*

I remember seeing a poster of a sleepy kitten sharing a small flowerpot with a large cactus. The caption read: "When we are at peace with ourselves, anywhere can be home." When we realize that serenity comes from within, we no longer depend on life remaining constant to feel at peace. In fact, change is the only constant in life. Without it, we would cease to grow.

Change can definitely be stressful if we don't change our thinking. But when we align our thinking with the changes in our life, it can be interesting and even fun. Fighting change with our thoughts creates stress. To paraphrase an old Hindu proverb: "If a fish swims up the mountain stream, it will be bruised against the rocks, exhaust itself, and dislike the journey. If the fish swims with the current, however, it easily avoids the rocks, travels swiftly, and enjoys the journey. The stream doesn't care which way the fish swims."

Neither does life. When we accept that change is inevitable, we feel at peace again. When we realize how the mind works, we can go with the flow of life rather than against it and stop creating unnecessary stress for ourselves.

I used to believe that I had to be in control of life—my relationships, my career, and all the events surrounding them. I had a preconceived map of life and if it wasn't going the way I expected, which it never did, I felt frustrated, angry, and stressed. Once I understood the role my thinking plays in creating my experience, I began to see and accept the perfect way my life is unfolding. Life is now an adventure, no longer a battle against all odds. Change makes life interesting.

MYTH #6: *Getting stress off your chest helps to reduce it.*

If this were true there would be no stress in the addictions field. We are so good at complaining about stress that we don't realize that we are validating it as we talk. In Twelve-Step groups we often do the same thing and wonder why, when we leave, we sometimes feel worse than when we came.

Whenever we talk about stress in a way that leads to self-pity we diminish our power to change ourselves and our environment. Sometimes we can see the problem, but it is not until our level of understanding changes that we see the solution.

When stress is relieved, our perspective and wisdom return, allowing us to see that the stress was self-created and showing us how to make our work (parenting, housecleaning, finances, and so forth) go more easily.

The theory that thinking about stress is a good idea reinforces the notion that stress is something you catch from "out there." Believing this reduces us to victims of circumstance. When we recognize our power in creating stress, we become free to eliminate it.

This doesn't mean that we won't have problems in life. As a friend of mine once said, "Life is like a contact sport. If you want to play the game, you will get your bumps. But, if you understand thought, you'll roll with the punches."

Stress—the Signal to Slow Down

The emotions associated with stress are part of the internal warning system that tells me when it is time to quiet the mind and slow down—take my focus off the details—until I regain my sense of serenity. Sometimes I become aware of stress through a physical sensation such as muscle tension, stomachaches, or clumsiness. If I heed the warning and let go of the thoughts surrounding it, the discomfort will diminish; if not, it will worsen until I pay attention. People who ignore these signals get sick, have high blood pressure, and miss a lot of work. Wouldn't it be better to catch it earlier?

Don't judge yourself when you become aware that you are stressed. Realize you can learn from the experience and drop another belief that is creating a blind spot in your life.

The Cycle of Stress

The diagram on the next page may help to summarize the cycle of stress and the steps we often innocently take to create it.

Living without Stress

Many of the Jews who were released from the concentration camps after World War II initially felt guilty for surviving while millions of others had died. Freed from external threat or hopeless conditions, many continued to create an internal hell. You would think that the survivors would be grateful and exuberant. Yet quite often, human beings who are used to living at a certain level of unhappiness have a hard time letting go of the habit of negative thinking.

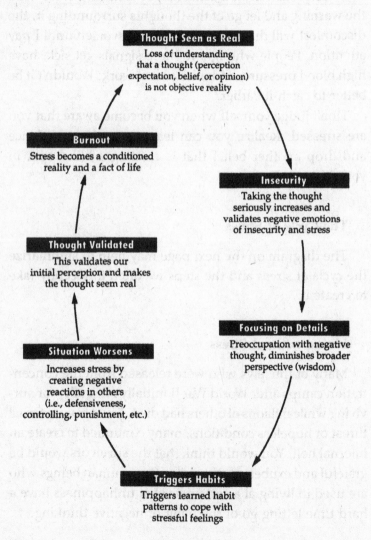

Cycle of Stress

Thought Seen as Real
Loss of understanding that a thought (perception expectation, belief, or opinion) is not objective reality

Insecurity
Taking the thought seriously increases and validates negative emotions of insecurity and stress

Focusing on Details
Preoccupation with negative thought, diminishes broader perspective (wisdom)

Triggers Habits
Triggers learned habit patterns to cope with stressful feelings

Situation Worsens
Increases stress by creating negative reactions in others (i.e., defensiveness, controlling, punishment, etc.)

Thought Validated
This validates our initial perception and makes the thought seem real

Burnout
Stress becomes a conditioned reality and a fact of life

This is one of the most common causes of setbacks and relapse with my clients. They can't get used to having a nice life, especially since they aren't really doing anything to deserve it. We are creatures of habit, and we must gradually grow accustomed to a serene, stress-free existence.

We see others who are still caught up in the myths of stress and we sometimes doubt our new insights. Misery loves company and if we begin showing a happy face to co-workers or family and friends, they often attempt to pressure us back to our old patterns of behavior. When this occurs, it is important to remember the adage: "Mind your own business."

An intern at our clinic changed dramatically in her approach to her job as an inpatient chemical dependency counselor when she came to understand the principles of Psychology of Mind. She began to enjoy her counseling and took a special interest in each client. She didn't get involved in the staff griping sessions. At first, the other staff thought she didn't care about them anymore, or that she had been born again, or that maybe she was using drugs.

She weathered these storms and people saw that she had really changed. Little by little, they began seeking her advice, and they began to be more positive in their work, too. The whole unit has benefited. She was wise in that she never tried to influence their thinking directly—she just minded her own business.

Cycle of Stress-Free Living

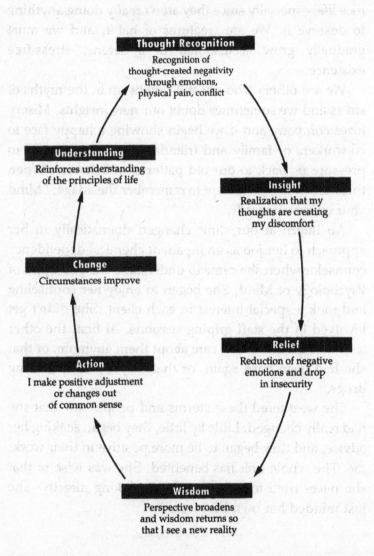

Thought Recognition
Recognition of
thought-created negativity
through emotions,
physical pain, conflict

Insight
Realization that my
thoughts are creating
my discomfort

Understanding
Reinforces understanding
of the principles of life

Relief
Reduction of negative
emotions and drop
in insecurity

Change
Circumstances improve

Action
I make positive adjustment
or changes out
of common sense

Wisdom
Perspective broadens
and wisdom returns so
that I see a new reality

When we mind our own business, we see that the greatest power we have to influence others is by changing ourselves. When one person finds serenity and lives in a stress-free state, it is an inspiration to others. If I encounter someone in my world who is happy, it makes me look at how I am responsible for creating my own unhappiness.

We must have the courage to mind our own business, our own state of mind. We cannot blame others if we lose our positive feeling—it will only perpetuate the illusion that the power to change is external rather than within. When we turn inside for our source of strength, it is always there.

Chapter 10

RELATIONSHIPS AND
ADDICTIONS

Chances are, most of us will interact with an addict sometime in our lives. Regardless of our relationship—spouse, parent, sibling, friend, or employee—our mental health is not contingent on the addict or his/her changes.

Nevertheless, as long as we seek serenity from external sources, we will be involved in controlling, manipulating, wishing, suffering, blaming, analyzing, and avoiding—behaviors common to people who identify themselves with addicts. In fact, the illusion that our identities revolve around another person is the heart of the concept of codependency—and our current misunderstanding of addictive family systems. When we bind our identities and self-worth to our mission to reform the addict, we are seeking happiness through external forces just as surely as the addict is through his addiction.

"If he would change I'd be happy." "If I could get her to quit drinking, I would have done something worthwhile in life, and then I'd be more worthwhile." "If my kid would just grow up, I wouldn't have to worry about her all the time." These thoughts create emotions like resentment, guilt, judgment, superiority, and sadness. They keep us tied to the past and the future and prevent us from living in the precious present, the only place in time where serenity can be experienced.

Family Delusions—A Case of Separate Realities

Like addicts, their family members are victims of thought systems that trap them in separate realities of conditioned belief. Until we realize the principle of thought as a voluntary function and the fact of separate realities, we cannot see beyond our delusions.

When we feel insecure—the common feeling in an addictive system—our egos go full steam ahead as we try to think our way out of uncomfortable situations. The more we think, the more we are ensnared in the web of delusions that obscures the truth of our wisdom. In the process, we sacrifice feelings of self-esteem and serenity as we drift further and further from the Self.

Insecurity is the prevalent feeling in addicted family relationships. Quite often, addicts blame those around them for their behavior, creating an atmosphere of mistrust and paranoia. Rigidity and perfectionism are common. So are physical and sexual abuse. These patterns all build insecurity, the breeding ground for maladaptive and negative behavior. Insecurity is expressed, by both addicts and their intimates, through behaviors ranging from super-achieving to extreme antisocial behavior, which become a false ego identity that masks feelings of insecurity from others and from ourselves. Because of the nature of the thought system, however, the thinking patterns we develop to lessen our insecurity actually perpetuate it. When the level of understanding remains the same, the thought system cannot break out of its present frame of reference. It only deceives us into thinking we have changed when we have simply reshuffled the hand we're already holding.

Consider Tommy, whose father is an alcoholic. Tommy tries to gain his father's approval—and his own security—by succeeding in sports and in school. No matter how well he does on the hockey rink or a math test, however, he always fears he won't be able to keep it up. This fear fosters more insecurity, so Tommy tries harder. No amount of success in the world can make Tommy feel secure, because you can't earn security—you already have it, unless you believe you don't.

Tommy is like the proverbial donkey with the carrot dangling just out of reach of his head. Tommy's search for approval is also attached to his head—to his thinking—and thus can never be permanently satisfied.

No Escape through Thinking

Many spouses and children of addicts think they can escape the pain and suffering of living with an addict through divorce or running away. Unfortunately, their thought systems are part of the baggage. Until we regain responsibility for our thinking through understanding we will repeat the same destructive patterns at home and on the job.

Take Mary, for example. Her mom, an alcoholic, had many love affairs which Mary shielded from her father, an enabler who seemed oblivious to the situation. Mary adopted her dad's pattern and later married an alcoholic. After several years of suffering the consequences of her husband's drinking, she divorced him and immediately fell in love with Phil, who was drug and alcohol dependent. Although Mary didn't deliberately seek out addicts, she clearly was attracted to them. The relationship with Phil lasted a few years. Then Mary went to Alanon and was told that her unhappiness and physical problems stemmed from living with a chemically dependent person. Although she eventually got Phil into treatment through an intervention, the relationship lost its appeal and within six months she divorced him.

Mary was determined not to marry another chemically dependent person. Then she met Roger. He was different in that he was recovering with ten years of sobriety. She felt she had finally met the man of her dreams. He was very affectionate and was involved in his AA group. All went smoothly for a couple of years until Mary discovered that Roger was sleeping with his fellow group members and was addicted to sex.

At this point Mary came to counseling and began learning the principles of Psychology of Mind. Gradually, she felt better and discovered that her mental health wasn't dependent on her husband. She came to see that her thinking kept the past alive and that her fears created a self-fulfilling prophecy. As she began to see her own innocence and that of her husband, her resentments and guilt dissolved. As she started to change, Roger came to counseling and as he developed some understanding, his affairs and desire for other women came to a halt.

Until Mary understood the source of her reality, she was stuck with the product of her thinking. Once she realized the power of her ability to think, she changed her state of mind and her world followed suit.

Mary is typical of so many people who have grown up in a reality where addictive patterns are learned. They search for a way out of the emotional pain through an intellectual path that always leads back to the original pattern of thought, thus averting the possibility of change. Until a higher level of understanding goes to work on insecurity, no real change will take place.

The Science of Letting Go

Earlier in my life, as a family therapist working with addicted family systems and as a member of Alanon, I often heard and used the term "let go." It was easy enough to say but very difficult to do. When I first attended a seminar on Psychology of Mind, I immediately realized that here was the key to a scientific and practical understanding of how to let go.

Letting go means taking attention and thoughts off a particular person, event, or behavior. In addiction's language, it usually means to stop controlling the behavior of others or ourselves. When we can't let go, we can't quit thinking about it. We don't recognize that we are doing the thinking and believe that others need to change before we can feel better. In fact, it is only when we drop our negative thoughts that we feel better.

Take Peter, for example, who said he wouldn't be happy until his wife Jane quit drinking. Once she did stop, he still felt bad because he couldn't trust her abstinence. In both situations, his thinking was producing his unhappiness. The choice is ours; when we choose to let go of our negative thoughts, our natural serenity will surface. Once we recognize that we are thinking, we are free to choose whether to be happy or to be right—right about worrying, being angry, hurt, or any other negative emotion.

Being right isn't winning when it diminishes the love and respect in our relationships. When we stop trying to analyze, manipulate, or fix the addict, we see that he is responsible for his own change. When we stop trying to find our salvation in others, we perceive that it is within us. When we realize the principle of thought as a voluntary function, we see that our thought system doesn't have to control us as we once believed. Once we see through the "grand illusion"—that trying to control others can cure them of their addiction—we see that happiness can only come from within us. We also understand that other people who are acting insecure are doing so innocently and need compassion and understanding, not judgment.

The cornerstone of recovery is to realize that we are responsible for our happiness, free to create whatever life we choose. If we truly want to be happy, we must be willing to let go of guilt, resentment, and other negative thoughts associated with the past. The past is over. It is an illusion. Accordingly, we must drop our identities as victims of past relationships and let common sense guide us toward an intimacy with others that is not based on insecurity or need, but rather on love and understanding.

The Impact of Serenity on Relationships

As we come to understand the principles of psychological functioning, our relationships take on a whole new form. When we feel secure, we can better distinguish who is responsible for what in a relationship. For example, we stop feeling guilty for others' shortcomings or behavior even if they tell us we are responsible. When we stop playing games, so must they—or they must find other playmates. It takes two to tango.

When we feel serene and secure we are naturally more open, respectful, and loving toward others. There is no need for defensiveness or blame because we are at peace with ourselves and the ego is not trying to protect its image. We are able to appreciate others' positive characteristics and feel compassionate when they are insecure and behaving negatively. We are patient with others' changes and let go of our need to control them so we can feel good. Although we want to help others realize their own serenity, we know we can't do it for them. Above all, we see beyond others' insecure habits to their inner goodness. As we recognize it, they are encouraged to recognize it too.

Changing the World

One common characteristic of so-called codependent people is the desire to change the world. It is not a bad idea, but they go about it backward. The way to change the world is to find peace of mind for ourselves. My friend, Dr. Keith Blevens of Baylor University, wrote a story regarding one of his clients who was married to an alcoholic. I will relay the story in its entirely because it so clearly illustrates the point:

I was reminded of a woman who entered psychotherapy very depressed. Her marriage of fifteen years was in shambles. She was married to an alcoholic. After a few visits, however, she entered the office one day and announced, "I've realized something! Something I had never known, really, until now. When I change, the world changes!"

"What do you mean?" I asked.

"I mean I have been going to various meeting for over twelve years trying to get help for my husband, Taylor, and myself— but I had completely missed the simple truth of change until now.

"Last Saturday afternoon I was cooking macaroni," she related. "It started to get late, and Taylor wasn't home yet. I knew he was drinking again because every other time he has been late, he has been drinking, and I thought, this won't be different.

"I started remembering the past and the burden it had been being married to Taylor, how he had abused himself and me. The more I thought about it, the more depressed and angry I got.

"I thought about all the complaining, threats, arguments, and fights we had been through. I felt overwhelmed; I began to cry. My tears dripped into the macaroni.

"Suddenly, it hit me—this has nothing to do with Taylor. These feelings have to do with me and my own thinking. What was I doing?

"Standing alone in my kitchen, I had succeeded in making myself perfectly miserable. And the best part is I actually realized—I understood—that I had been creating this kind of turmoil within myself all my life. Over and over again, in count-less ways, I have turned my own thoughts and feelings against myself.

"You know, I have worked so hard for so long for change, but I have been going about it backwards. I have been focusing my thoughts on my problems, so that I could find an answer and then change them.

"Well, for twelve years I have been thinking about my prob-lems, and I have been missing all the fun and joy of life. I have been as addicted to focusing on my problems as Taylor has been to alcohol.

"I see clearly now that what I think about creates my feelings—

and that I can change my mind and thought to create a better world for myself. I realized Taylor was not the problem and I didn't have to wait for him to change for me to feel better."

She felt so good after these insights that she was quite happy when Taylor arrived, even though he had been drinking. "For once," she said, "that didn't stop me." It mattered little in the face of her newfound insight and understanding. At first, Taylor was taken aback by the strength of her happiness. She had to chuckle to herself, noticing his initial suspicion of her good feelings.

As they talked and began to interact, he became endearing to her in new ways. She felt a deep sense of love for him and for his being there. She saw beyond his insecurities, even beyond his alcoholism, and her own judgments, fear, and anger. She enjoyed talking to him as never before in their marriage.

That evening after dinner, they sat at the kitchen table for hours, talking, crying, and laughing together. Neither of them had ever experienced such beautiful heart-to-heart communication.

After her insight, this client and her relationship with her loved one changed completely. Once she understood how her mind worked via thought to create reality, she knew how change could happen.

After this, her anger and despondency subsided. She found she no longer wanted or needed to give herself such negative feelings. She developed a sense of self-respect for the value of her own positive feelings and thoughts.

Taylor also changed. He began to like being home again; he, too, began to feel happier, better. He started to enjoy his life and family. His alcohol abuse first slowed, then stopped completely.

That was nearly three years ago. Most important, these have been years of happiness for them both.[7]

This example shows the power of a true insight into how thought creates reality. When we realize the power of thought, we quit trying to change the world in a backwards fashion. Rather, we understand how to "let go with love" and thus get off the merry-go-round of painful relationships with addicts.

Chapter 11

PREVENTING RELAPSE

Relapse is a major issue in the addiction field today. Chemical dependency professionals shied away from this topic for years because we wanted to recognize our successes, not our failures. We tended to blame the power of the "disease." As our profession evolved, however, research on rates of relapse revealed problems too blatant to ignore. Relapse is not something to be denied, but to be understood.

Relapse rate statistics are available primarily for alcoholism. The research is quite dramatic. In a major study, George Valliant found that among a group of one hundred alcoholics treated by hospital detoxification programs, compulsory AA attendance, and an active follow-up program, 95 percent relapsed.[8] In another study, Emerick and Hansen reported that 93 percent of alcoholics who had been treated returned to drinking within four years.[9] Valliant also found that the 5 percent who did abstain from alcohol commonly formed alternate addictions. Most treatment centers report significantly better results although their follow-up period is generally much shorter.

Clearly, treatment isn't working. That is not surprising since most treatment has focused solely on the addictive behavior and not on teaching people to tap into their own health and serenity.

Serenity is the antidote to relapse, dry drunks, and transfer of addictions. When we begin recovery, we often think it is enough if we are not practicing our addiction. But just as physical health is more than the absence of disease, recovery is more than the absence of addictive behavior. The only way we can ensure freedom from addiction is if we learn to comply with the principles of psychological functioning, which return us to our innate state of serenity.

Relapse is an opportunity for self-discovery, not cause for shame. If we judge ourselves for relapsing, we will remain stuck in the quicksand of guilt, hopelessness, and negativity. Or, we can use relapse as an opportunity to move toward the truth. If we are open, patient, and humble, we will evolve with each faltering step. The choice is ours.

The Causes of Relapse, Dry Drunks, and Transfer of Addictions

I often hear recovering addicts say that they are abstinent, but not happy. Their recovery is a struggle and they believe it must be taken very seriously. They have learned to distrust their motives, yet they long to feel better. They are often preoccupied with addiction in themselves and in others. They experience insecurity, which manifests as depression, envy, self-pity, self-consciousness, and fear.

One cause of relapse is inflated self-importance or ego pride. When we hold our noses too high, we trip over our own feet. Another cause is the tendency to be brittle or rigid in our beliefs and inflexible toward other people's realities, which can lead to a breakdown of positive feelings.

Before relapse or transfer of addictions can occur, the internal psychological climate must be right. Just as the atmosphere must present specific conditions for lightning to strike, a person must be in a lowered level of understanding for relapse to happen.

There are five main causes of relapse: focusing on the past; focusing on details; trying to pump up the ego; relying on rituals and techniques; and the belief that you need to "get out" negative feelings. The next sections cover the guidelines that can be taken to prevent each.

Guideline #1: Living in the Present

As I discussed in the chapter on myths, it is not necessary or helpful to pick apart the mistakes of the past in order to avoid repeating them. You cannot drive your car forward by staring in the rearview mirror. It is necessary at times to check the rearview mirror, however, to make sure nothing from the past is bearing down on you or to catch another glimpse of something wonderful. We will, of course, feel sadness at times and may pass through several transitions in our acceptance of loss. But it is dangerous to codify or ritualize our approach to loss, or we risk getting stuck in the past.

Many people spend years working through family of origin issues. Told that they will never be completely free of the past, recovering addicts go from one therapist to another, forming a dependency on therapy itself. This practice is very harmful to the recovery process.

I recently received a letter from a recovered alcoholic who had learned about the principles of Psychology of Mind from books and tapes. He had relapsed four times in three years and was in long-term treatment as a last resort. He was marked by a great deal of emotional scar tissue from growing up with two alcoholic parents and physical abuse. In treatment, he was forced to relive his painful childhood memories. Each time, he felt more stuck and frustrated and subsequently returned to drinking. He said the understanding of how to let go of the past gave him a second chance in life. What follows is an excerpt from his letter:

I am trying to be neither cruel nor sarcastic when I say that in all of the programs I was in and even in private counseling, the counselors seemed almost delighted to hear about my difficult childhood. I think this was because they considered the roots of my problem to be clearly exposed so they would have no difficulty in getting to them. Time and again I was asked to dig down deep inside and regurgitate as many bad memories as possible and feel again all the emotions that went with the thoughts. Oddly enough, and for reasons that never made sense to me, this was called "facing the problem."

Two weeks prior to my first contact with Psychology of Mind, I was getting extra points in a "grief group" if I could shed tears. The relief that was evident on the faces of the counselors at the successful completion of this feat convinced me of one thing. These people honestly thought that this was going to help me be happy today. And I did feel better for a while. Just doing something that pleased the professionals and my fellow recovering people sparked a flame of hope that something would finally click with me, too.

But I had been trying this same therapy for four years and I knew nothing was different. It was only leading me back to a road of pain and despair. When I followed my heart and my common sense and became tired of this constant request for pain, I rebelled and quit looking backwards. I told the group and the counselors that I was not going to be a slave to my past anymore. I was immediately labeled as being "in denial" and a case of "self will run riot."[10]

Two weeks later I read a book and listened to tapes on Psychology of Mind. When I realized what was happening to me and that I really had a right to my own wisdom and, yes, my own spirit, I cried and literally exploded inside with a warmth and flood of positive feelings that I will never forget. I can also say with all honesty that I still experience this feeling to some extent each day. By realizing that thought is only a function, something that we human beings do as naturally as breathing, I took the power away from my past and let it slide back into the river of time that flows behind us as we journey through our lives. As easily as I can extract the good thoughts and memories which create love and joy, I can also dismiss the negative thoughts that create insecurity, jealousy, and despair.

It is here that I would like to quote James Allen from his book *As a Man Thinketh*. "Man is made or unmade by himself: in the armory of thought he forges the weapons by which he destroys himself; he also fashions the tools with which he builds for himself heavenly mansions of joy and strength and peace. By the right choices and true application of thought man ascends to the divine perfection."[11]

The most fulfilling thought for me today when I read this is that what I once read and possessed as knowledge within my mind is now a feeling of understanding in my heart, and the distance between the two is growing smaller every day.[12]

When we dub the past a reality rather than memory, we breathe life into it and experience it as if it were now. The same is true of planning too much for tomorrow or projecting failure and worry about what might be. Both past and future are illusions of thought—not realities.

Serenity and wisdom can only be realized in the present. Whenever you become embroiled in past memories or future worries, remember that this moment is the only one that truly exists.

When we are living in the present, we can respond with wisdom and clarity, moving through life without stress. Change takes place effortlessly and we see life unfold miraculously before our eyes. We see the beauty in nature, our family and friends, and ourselves, and our natural response is gratitude. We never are given more than we can handle in life unless we use our thought system to project us into the future and the past and become overwhelmed.

Living in the present does not mean we never recall the past or plan for the future. It means that we do so only when it is necessary or enjoyable. In a higher level of understanding we access our thought system for significant information like phone numbers, birthdays, or to plan for a holiday or balance the checkbook. In this higher state we do not use thought against ourselves by probing the details of past problems or lamenting the possibilities of the future. Our emotions will let us know if our thinking becomes self-destructive so that we can forestall forecasting or reminiscing.

I once had a client who just had completed chemical dependency treatment. Upon his return home, he started to mull over the past and all the hurt he had caused his wife and children during his drinking days. Soon he was depressed and preoccupied with guilt. His wife and kids had forgiven him and were glad to have him home and sober for the first time in years. But his state of mind kept him from seeing their love for him, and he interpreted any requests as accusations that he was not being a good father or husband. His state of mind continued to plummet and self-pity set in. At this point he realized he wanted to drink again and came to therapy with me.

He learned to recognize his negative thinking and drop it, and he started to see his life in terms of the present. He became grateful for his sobriety, health, and loving family. His desire to drink faded as his level of understanding rose.

Guideline #2: Simplicity

When we realize the simplicity of the principles of psychological functioning, the details of our personalities and circumstances fall into harmony like the individual instruments of a symphony orchestra under the watchful guidance of a skillful conductor. Wisdom gives us a higher perspective to view the total picture of our lives.

Recovering addicts often get so busy trying to master all the details of their lives that they forget to enjoy themselves. Recovery becomes another weighty project to be carried out in meticulous detail. The trouble is, if we master the details but lose our feeling of serenity in the process, we will create yet more details to tackle. We must give ourselves a K.I.S.S.—Keep It Simple, Stupid. We can't fix our personalities through analysis. It is only when we achieve a higher level of understanding and a tranquil mind that the symphony conductor emerges with the simple and obvious way to put life in order. When we discover the simplicity of life's principles, we are able to ignore the yammering of our ego mind and listen to our innate common sense.

We often lose track of simplicity due to the modern-day propensity to label the personality passive-aggressive, codependent, narcissistic, compulsive, or adult child of an alcoholic. All these descriptions keep us focused on a false self rather than the true identity that lies beyond the personality.

The word *personality* comes from the Greek word for "mask." We are not the mask but the being behind the mask, or the creator of all experience. If we want growth or change, we must understand that we are not our personalities, labels, feelings, or thoughts. We are the power that creates them, our consciousness makes them seem real.

Guideline #3: Natural Self-Esteem

People often leave treatment with an "I'll show 'em" attitude. To rebuild their self-esteem they try to prove themselves through a variety of accomplishments: recouping financial losses, rebuilding a business, finding a new spouse, or earning a one-year sobriety pin. There is nothing wrong with these accomplishments when they are an outgrowth of natural self-esteem. When motivated by ego-building, however, these efforts are sure to end in disaster. The problem occurs when human beings become driven to prove themselves.

We are conditioned to believe that self-esteem must be earned through hard work. Conditional self-esteem means waiting until we reach our goals to feel good about ourselves. We tend to judge ourselves against others or against how we think we should be progressing, which inevitably leads to feelings of disappointment, self-doubt, "analysis paralysis," jealousy, and arrogance. These feelings all lower our state of mind to create fertile soil for the dry-drunk syndrome and relapse. Trying to reconstruct a broken ego is like building on a foundation of sand. Solid recovery is built on the bedrock of natural self-esteem. Self-esteem is our birthright, a part of serenity. We don't have to earn it or work for it. It is there when we accept it. Natural self-esteem is unconditional. When we accept and love ourselves—regardless of where we are in our growth—we think less about ourselves. We live in the present and become more aware of life around us.

Children who are loved with no strings attached are likely to experience this natural self-esteem. They are not driven to prove themselves and yet they often accomplish a tremendous amount in life. On the other hand, children raised with conditional love (manipulation through affection, which really isn't love at all) learn to like themselves for what they do, and are driven to accomplish or are defiantly opposed to doing anything at all. Self-love, or self-esteem, is no different. Conditional self-love breeds defiance and compulsion. Unconditional self-love breeds wisdom and health.

Guideline #4: Inspiration and Common Sense

In our effort to recover, we often take our clues from successful predecessors. Unfortunately, we tend to watch what they do rather than understand how they do it. If we are feeling insecure or mistrust our inner guidance, we may emulate the action of others, even though it doesn't feel right. The result is a ritual. That is, we are doing some activity (jogging, reading a particular book, attending a particular class) because we believe it is necessary to find peace of mind.

When we perform a ritual, we are looking to the outside for a feeling that is within. Our feeling (wisdom) may be telling us to do something quite the opposite of the ritual; and if we don't know to trust it, we will impede our progress. We will know whether we are acting ritualistically or out of inspiration by the way it makes us feel. If it is inspired, it will feel right. Sometimes in the beginning it is hard to tell which is which. But, little by little, we become more sensitive to our inner guidance — and learn to hone our skill of listening within for the answers.

What might be just the course for one recovering person may harm another. Making rules for recovery is like being directed by an inaccurate map. If instead we direct ourselves toward common sense, each of us will find his or her own unique way.

Timing is so important with anything in life. If we plant seeds too early in the spring we endanger the young plants. The same is true for recovery. For example, for some people, to go to a group twice a week may be extremely helpful at one point in their recovery. At another time, it may be better to take a break from the group or stop attending altogether.

A bulemic client told me she was interested in taking a dance class. She loved to dance and was drawn to the class. The experience gave her a new sensitivity and respect for her body. She said her body "screamed" at her to quit vomiting. This new awareness was a beginning step for her to see her body as a friend, not an enemy. Going to dance class was not my idea; for others with eating disorders, it might even have been harmful. But, as her counselor, my job was to teach her to trust her own feeling. She did, and the result was just right for her.

People often make another mistake. They use a technique or ritual that is very helpful at first, until it becomes a habit. They begin looking to the ritual or technique for their positive feelings rather than looking within. They repeat the ritual frequently and it still doesn't work. Doing something uninspired and looking to the outside for happiness will feel empty and compulsive; that means we should quit doing it.

Guideline #5: Positive Feelings as a Guide Toward Serenity

If I wanted to go to the North Pole, I would not travel east, west, or south. I would check my compass and head due north. If I want to find serenity, I must look in the right direction, too. Serenity is not a negative feeling; it is a positive feeling of harmony, love, gratitude, and tranquility. If we believe we must express our negative emotions in order to experience positive feelings, we are headed south to go north.

As I discussed in chapter 6, our emotions are a built-in feedback mechanism that lets us know our state of mind. Emotions tell us if our thoughts are expressions of our belief system—products of past conditioning—or if they stem from our common sense.

Everything we think is expressed in one form or another. Consequently, the more we believe in a thought, the more expression we give it in our lives. That expression often takes the form of emotions, for every thought creates an immediate emotional response. As you'll remember, this response tells us the direction that thought is taking us. If we ignore these signals, the expression of our thought gets "louder." That is, it will become a behavior that produces a reaction from the outer world and the cycle may start again. If the thought is a false belief, life will indicate as much in the form of pain or misfortune. This is life's way of showing us that our thinking is on the wrong track. As we learn how thought creates our reality, however, we can recognize a false belief earlier, nipping it in the bud before our actions take a turn for the worst.

The present emphasis on getting out all our negative emotions creates a great deal of unnecessary pain for clients and for those who must listen to their suffering. It is far better to patch the leaky canoe instead of continually bailing it out. We must stop the leak (negative thinking) before we can make any progress. Our emotions will guide us toward positivity. If you were walking through the woods you wouldn't go through the marshes or the thickets; you would follow the path of least resistance. So it is with our lives.

PART FOUR

The Future of Recovery

Chapter 12

THE IMPLICATIONS OF PSYCHOLOGY OF MIND FOR THE PREVENTION AND TREATMENT OF ADDICTIONS

The birth of a new idea is only the beginning. The idea must mature into reality. Our evolution as human beings, as a science, and as a helping profession will emerge with greater degrees of our mental health. Our evolution will emerge as a willingness to accept something new; to listen to someone saying that the world is round rather than flat; that the earth is not the center of the solar system; that energy, matter, and space are related; or that perhaps by shifting our focus away from the manifestations of people's problems to the principles of thought, reality, consciousness, and emotions, we will see our connection to mental health. The simplicity of this new psychology has given us the means of helping people realize a cure for conditions that have been considered incurable. What this means to a society is that it has found the route to its own wisdom.

—*Sanity, Insanity, and Common Sense*

Try to imagine the implications of Psychology of Mind for the field of addictions and the treatment of mental illness. Just as it would have been difficult for peers of the Wright brothers to picture the skies filled with airliners, it is hard to imagine that this simple yet profound discovery of the nature of thought and reality will assist millions of people.

Along with many other professionals across the country who have used these principles, I have observed countless people who were once sentenced to lives of mental illness or addictions not only free themselves of symptoms but experience productivity and happiness. Once the Wright brothers broke the psychological/gravitational barrier and actually flew, it was only a matter of time until the rest of us caught up. We now take flying for granted. Although it may be difficult to accept at first, once a fact has been uncovered it is eventually incorporated into society's realm of knowledge.

Although we have come a long way since the early days of AA, the addictions field is still just getting off the ground. It has a collective belief system, as does any discipline of science or religion. Whenever an advance is made in our profession, we must have the courage to let go of our current ideas so that we can move forward in helping others. We must entertain the possibility that addictions can actually be prevented and cured, not just coped with and accepted.

Implications for Treatment

The evolution that Psychology of Mind represents means that treatment of addictions no longer has to be a long, painful process of therapy. Treatment facilities will become centers of positive care that go beyond teaching clients and their families to get rid of their compulsive habits to restore sanity and serenity. Serenity will not be seen as an end goal for the lucky few, but as a moment-to-moment state of mind that is always accessible.

Addiction counselors will understand that the only way to pass this knowledge on to their clients is to realize it in their own lives, to embody what they teach. As they find serenity and see increased results from their work, burnout will become a thing of the past. Stress will be seen as internally created, not "caught" like a virus. This will stop hundreds of people from leaving our profession.

The infighting and ego-based politics of treatment centers will be replaced by cooperative, harmonious cultures that change and develop readily in response to the changing needs of staff and client populations. Numerous health care facilities and businesses have already incorporated the principles of this new psychology into their management philosophy with excellent results in terms of increased morale, greater productivity, improved interpersonal relationships, and increased revenues.

Our treatment practices will be consistent, unified by a scientific and truthful understanding of how to guide people to mental health. Helping professionals will replace hundreds of variations of therapeutic concepts and techniques with common sense and wisdom.

Clients will be less resistant to treatment because it will be based on a positive feeling and will educate them about health, not just their addiction. Lightheartedness will set the tone for change and growth. Clients who used to be very resistant in my counseling practice now look forward to their sessions as informative, enlightening, and enjoyable. I feel the same way.

As a result of this new approach, relapse rates will drop. Recidivism is an outgrowth of ineffective treatment —not the nature of addiction. Just as more cancers are being cured with the development of better treatments, so will addictions be less likely to recur. As clients learn the principles of how to achieve serenity, they will have a more satisfying sobriety and will not need to search for other addictions to fill the void created by the absence of the old habit. When relapse does occur, it will not be seen as a failure, but rather as an opportunity to learn more.

The myths, or contaminants, in our current treatment practices cause a high incidence of divorce and family disruption. As addictions treatment deemphasizes past issues and negative emotions to focus on educating families in the principles, it will facilitate forgiveness and understanding. The result will be more harmony and positive feelings in the family, and fewer divorces.

Family members will enjoy new love and intimacy in an atmosphere that is secure and lighthearted. This will allow children to learn what security feels like. Children experiencing a secure family environment will have high self-esteem and internal direction. Consequently, they will be less prone to peer pressure to participate in self-destructive behavior. This will break the cycle of multigenerational addiction. Families will become nurturing, loving, and fun to be around, strengthening the family as a unit in our society.

In a paper presented to the annual conference of the Florida Alcohol and Drug Abuse Association, Charles Stewart reported on the efficacy of this therapy with court-mandated DWI clients.[13] The results were quite surprising. I knew that voluntary clients profited by this type of therapy and were highly motivated, but I wasn't sure how it would work with those forced to participate in lieu of prison.

Participants not only listened attentively and reported incorporating the principles in their lives; many volunteered for the course a second time, brought their spouses, and referred friends and co-workers to the program. Some clients were so interested in the approach that they elected to continue therapy even though their insurance would not cover the fee when it would cover other treatment facilities. Of the twenty-three subjects in the study, thirteen quit drinking completely, and all but one significantly moderated their drinking habits. Many reported changes in their level of stress related to work and family situations. Several clients said they quit drinking without realizing it until later. Their desire to feel good through drinking dropped off as they began to experience a natural state of mental health.

These results may sound too optimistic to be possible. They would have sounded that way to me at one time. But today they are realities for me, for my co-workers, and for numerous professional colleagues who are using this approach in hospitals, treatment centers, psychiatry, nursing, organizational counseling, and psychotherapy.

I know, beyond a shadow of a doubt, that the principles of Psychology of Mind offer possibilities for the realization of an ideal that has the power to transform our present definition of recovery and ultimately expand the illusionary limits we have placed on our attainment of mental health.

Implications for Prevention of Addictions

Ten years ago I worked as the director of primary prevention in a state alcoholism authority. We were often scoffed at because of the then-current belief that alcoholism was inherited and therefore unpreventable. Others believed that early intervention was the only viable prevention effort. Despite the resistance to prevention, we tried everything from "alternative highs," to nutrition and exercise programs, to responsible drinking campaigns, building family strength, self-esteem classes in the schools, and more.

What we didn't understand at the time was that prevention of maladaptive behaviors, such as drug abuse and alcoholism, was linked to mental health. More important, we didn't know what mental health was or how to elicit it.

Since that time Psychology of Mind has emerged, and we now see the relationship between a healthy state of mind and prevention of negative behaviors. We have solutions instead of more statistics on the problems. We know that mental health is a natural state in all human beings, and we can teach people how their minds work so they can direct themselves toward mental health. It is as if we have finally found the instruction manual to a machine we have been trying to use without knowing how. What a relief!

All human organisms have a genetic mapping, or heredity, that predisposes them to "break down" in certain predictable ways when exposed to stress. Stress makes some people prone to ulcers, alcoholism, or even psychosis. Without stress, these genetic tendencies would not be manifest. As we learn to live in serenity, we alleviate stress and avoid physical or mental breakdown. Thus, these principles function as a vaccination against addictions and mental illness, as well as numerous physical maladies.

Understanding how to maintain mental health and serenity is the antidote to addictions. Because these principles are simple and are based on the common sense we already have, they are relatively easy to teach and learn.

The future of primary prevention will be in discovering innovative ways to impart these principles to teachers, parents, children, health care professionals, and others who touch people's lives.

We are truly on the verge of rediscovering our own wisdom as a society. However, we must do this individual by individual. All of us have the possibility of uncovering our own wisdom. If we have the understanding that allows us to look within, we will unleash serenity. If we form an intent to put peace of mind ahead of all else, we will discover the power that lies within. When we understand how to let our thoughts become tranquil, we can distinguish habit from insight, ignorance from truth, selfishness from love. The power is ours to accept this understanding and follow it.

When we discover serenity for ourselves, we will be inspired to share it with others—our family, friends, and co-workers. We will become a beacon of hope.

For some of you, life may be chaotic and unhappy. Do not be discouraged. Seize any feeling of hope and trust it, for hope is the seed that will germinate a new life. Through the process of understanding the principles of psychological functioning, this seed will grow. Acquiring a solid foundation in the principles takes time and teaching. Don't worry about the speed of your progress. Know that you already have the wisdom and serenity you seek. Then relax and listen; let life and your teachers educate you.

NOTES

1. Rick Suarez, Roger C. Mills, Darlene Stewart, *Sanity, Insanity, and Common Sense: The Groundbreaking New Approach to Happiness* (New York: Fawcett Columbine, 1987).
2. William James, *The Principles of Psychology* (Cambridge, MA: Harvard University Press, 1981), p. 754.
3. Anonymous, "The Serenity Prayer" In Memorium column, *The New York Herald Tribune*, circa June 1941.
4. Nan Robertson, "The Changing World of Alcoholics Anonymous," *The New York Times Magazine*, Feb. 21, 1988, p. 57.
5. Nancy Magnuson, "Life Without a Label."
6. Annetta Miller, "Stress on the Job," *Newsweek*, April 25, 1988, p. 40.
7. Keith Blevens, "Changing the World," *The Phoenix* 6:8(1986):3.
8. George Valliant, *The Natural History of Alcoholism: Causes, Patterns, and Paths to Recovery* (Harvard University Press, 1983), p. 220.
9. C. D. Emerick, and J. Hansen, "Assertions regarding effectiveness of treatment for alcoholism: Fact or fantasy?" *American Psychologist* 38 (1983): 1078.
10. Anonymous, *Alcoholics Anonymous* (New York: Alcoholics Anonymous World Services, Inc., 1939), p. 62.
11. James Allen, *As a Man Thinketh* (White Plains, NY: Peter Pauper Press, Inc., n.d.), p. 9.
12. The author of this letter wishes to remain anonymous, but the letter is hereby printed with permission.

13. Charles Stewart, "The Efficacy of Neo-Cognitive Psychotherapy with DUI Clients." Paper delivered at the annual conference of the Florida Alcohol and Drug Abuse Association, Orlando, FL, October 2, 1987.

RESOURCES

Books

Banks, Syd. *In Quest of the Pearl*. Tampa, FL: Duval-Bibb, 1990.
Banks, Syd. *Second Chance*. Tampa, Fl: Duval-Bill, 1989.
Pransky, George. *How To Save Your Marriage*. HSI/Tab Books —
    a division of McGraw-Hill, 1990 (in press).

Tapes

Bailey, Joseph. *Two-Dimensional Recovery*. Minneapolis, MN:
    Minneapolis Institute of Mental Health, 1989.
Crystal, Amy. *Listening and the Process of Change*. Tampa, FL:
    Duval-Bibb, 1985.
Pransky, George. *Quality of Life*. (Twelve video tapes), LaCon-
    ner, WA: 1989.
Stewart, Darlene, and Charles Stewart. *Can Love Survive Com-
    mitment?* Tampa, FL: Duval-Bibb, 1989.

Books and tapes available at the Minneapolis Institute of Mental
Health, Ltd., 1409 Willow Street, Suite 500, Minneapolis, MN
55403. Telephone: 612-870-1084.

Books and tapes available at the Minneapolis Institute of Mental Health, Ltd., 1409 Willow Street, Suite 510, Minneapolis, MN 55403. Telephone: 612–870–1084.